SHUT UP AND READ

SHUT UP AND READ

A MEMOIR FROM HARRIETT'S BOOKSHOP

JEANNINE A. COOK

AMISTAD

An Imprint of HarperCollinsPublishers

How We Stay Free: Notes on a Black Uprising edited by Christopher R. Rogers, Fajr Muhammad, and the Paul Robeson House & Museum © 2022 Common Notions. Reprinted with the permission of Common Notions Press. All rights reserved.

Names have been changed to protect the privacy and identity of individuals portrayed in this book.

Without limiting the exclusive rights of any author, contributor or the publisher of this publication, any unauthorized use of this publication to train generative artificial intelligence (AI) technologies is expressly prohibited. HarperCollins also exercise their rights under Article 4(3) of the Digital Single Market Directive 2019/790 and expressly reserve this publication from the text and data mining exception.

SHUT UP AND READ. Copyright © 2026 by Jeannine Cook. All rights reserved. No part of this book may be used or reproduced in any manner whatsoever without written permission except in the case of brief quotations embodied in critical articles and reviews. For information, address HarperCollins Publishers, 195 Broadway, New York, NY 10007. In Europe, HarperCollins Publishers, Macken House, 39/40 Mayor Street Upper, Dublin 1, D01 C9W8, Ireland.

HarperCollins books may be purchased for educational, business, or sales promotional use. For information, please email the Special Markets Department at SPsales@harpercollins.com.

hc.com

FIRST EDITION

Designed by Jason Kayser

Library of Congress Cataloging-in-Publication Data has been applied for.

ISBN 978-0-06-342823-2

Printed in the United States of America

26 27 28 29 30 LBC 5 4 3 2 1

SHUT UP AND READ

SECTION I:
JULY 2024

Jeannine A. Cook interviews Sonia Sanchez

JEANNINE A. COOK: Mama Sonia, what are we getting right? And where are we missing the mark?

SONIA SANCHEZ: I am not sure we should start with right and wrong. But what I will say is we are not coming together the way we used to come together.

Chapter 1

I refuse to die with this story stuck in me. And now my doctor wants to slice open my throat. She instructs me to hold my head back. "You've been on this medicine for far too long," she says. "You need surgery," she says. It's been fourteen years, she says as she checks my throat.

"NO," I say for the fourteenth year in a row. "Give me liberty or give me death." I joke off her warnings even though it's hard to laugh with someone's hands around your neck.

Dr. Hahn makes the muscles in my shoulders tighten. She makes my heart race. And the hairs on my neck stand up. She's been wanting to have a piece of me for years. But once she starts cutting, who knows where she'll stop.

I breathe in good thoughts like my favorite story's ending. I like books to end smooth but not hokie. Soothing yet restrained.

I breathe out bad thoughts like Dr. Hahn with a scalpel in her left hand and my throat in the right. Blood vessels bursting. Bandages and pain.

"Your body is at war with itself," Dr. Hahn continues.

That means either way I win. I roll my eyes and smile.

"Your pressure's high. Your eyes are bulging. The tremors are back. These things can kill you," she nags me in her naggingly high voice. "We love you, Ms. Cook, and your books and your bookshops. We don't want to lose all you've built just like that." She snaps.

I can't tell her sarcasm from savior complex or pity from placation. Either way I pretend to ignore her.

A part of me wants to cut Dr. Hahn with her own blade and the other part wants to hug her and ask her to mother me and tell me everything will be okay. I tell both parts to hush up. We ain't doing this today. We have work to do. Take a deep breath, tell a joke, get the script, and get to the bookshops.

"What if dying is making me invincible?" I joke, hopping off Dr. Hahn's exam table. She doesn't laugh. She doesn't respond. She doesn't even smile. She's too afraid of the numbers on her chart. She's too afraid of death and dying. She calls herself a doctor but doesn't know that laughter is the best medicine. Sometimes I laugh because life is funny, and sometimes I laugh because life is like a tap on the funny bone.

"What if dying is making you insane?" Dr. Hahn cocks back.

"Your office is insanely cold, Dr. Hahn," I jab. "It smells sterile in here, too, like hospital sheets." I Joe Frazier bob and weave. We both laugh. Dr. Hahn makes me feel funny. I want to hear that I am okay. But she won't say that. I pull on my denim overalls before the exam is complete.

"The script?" I ask. We both know what I need. "Yes? No? Maybe so?"

She stares off. Flips through her charts and numbers. Checks my heart rate again and again. Says yes while shaking her head no. "You're killing me," she says. "You're always in flight. Eventually, you have to land. Take these pills as prescribed to get your levels down before surgery." An unexpected uppercut. She wins.

I nod in agreement. But she will not be cutting open my throat. The slightest mishap will leave me speechless, and I still have a few things I need to say. I pocket my script and agree, "Okay. Will take as needed. Okay."

"That's not what I said."

"But it's what I will do." I hold my crumpled prescription in a too-tight fist. "My body. My choice."

Dr. Hahn cracks another smile. It's a real one with straight teeth, pink gums, brushed, flossed—no decay.

We both let out a sigh of relief that the visit is almost complete. We tolerate one another, but we are not friends.

"And . . ." She pauses before I walk out.

"This is your last script. Next time I see you, it's for surgery." I thank her with a bow, put the crinkled prescription back in my pocket, and make it out of the Pennsylvania Hospital healthcare complex with enough time to open my bookshops for the day.

Chapter 2

It's July hot outside. I call my dad as I walk through the noise and funk of Philadelphia's SEPTA subway. His phone rings and rings. There's a blind musician singing "Ain't No Stopping Us Now" to the left of me and kids calling each other dickheads and young bulls to my right. It's pee and reefer smells everywhere. I appreciate the sounds of Philadelphia, but sometimes she stinks. It is her voice that sings sweet nothings in my wandering ear.

Philly called to me; I did not call her. I first arrived here twenty years ago, enticed by an accent of elongated a's and the replacing of proper nouns with improper "jawns." It was not love at first sight; it was love at first sound. I love her language.

It was my best friend, Marie, who really wanted to be with Philadelphia. I was just along for the ride and perhaps that's why I feel like a third wheel in my city. Philly was Marie's first love—not mine.

I always have a Marie. They are my guides. I believe everyone gets at least one Marie. If you listen to them, you get more. They take you places. I met my first Marie when I was eight years old. At seventeen, she was driving me from Hampton, Virginia, to Philadelphia to attend an open house at the college of *her* dreams.

That morning, we went to school as usual but skipped our last class, both complaining of the same stomachache. Gas was only ninety-nine cents a gallon and Allen Iverson, who'd just graduated from our high school, was now dominating as a center for Philadelphia's basketball team. Marie insisted that Iverson proved we could be from Hampton and move to Philly to be great.

She said let's drive her forest green stick shift up and back in one day, so our parents had no idea we'd been gone. "It's the city of brotherly love," Marie tells me as she plays Bilal, The Roots, Jill Scott, and Eve over and over during our five-hour car ride from the sandy beach shores of Virginia up north to the concrete jungle.

"We are visiting the esteemed University of the Arts. Built in 1876," she tells me. It is one of the oldest and finest art schools in the country, with colossal-sized Colosseum columns marking the entrance to the Avenue of the Arts on South Broad Street.

WELCOME TO THE FUTURE read a bright red banner as we ascended the stairs to Hamilton Hall.

Speak only when spoken to, I tell myself at most social events. I pick a seat in the corner to set up my paper and pen. I have decided I am just a silent observer at Marie's open house, so I am here to read the room.

I am only spoken to by one suited gentleman all evening. He comes up to me with a toothy grin. He speaks out of one side of his mouth and keeps one hand in his pocket.

"You're different," he says to me under his breath.

"No, I'm Jeannine," I say, still reading.

". . . but not in a bad way. You won't fit in *anywhere*," he continues, as if he were a fortune teller explaining my fate. "What are you reading?"

"Notes." I continued writing in my journal, describing his

scruffy five o'clock shadow, his oversized suit jacket, his balding hairline.

"What type of notes?"

"About people—what they're wearing, how they speak, how they move, their body language, what they say. It's like a game."

"You have notes about me?"

"I do," I reply.

"That's cool—a bit strange."

"Just something to pass the time."

"You don't seem too interested in the open house."

"It's alright, not my kind of place." The students had mohawks and colorful hair and piercings and tattoos and parents who were helping them fill out paperwork and portfolios and instruments and wide eyes and purposefully too-short bangs.

"I'm here with a friend," I said, pointing at Marie as she worked the room—smiling and shaking hands.

After asking me a bunch of questions, he continued with his fortune telling, like he was trying to sell me a cure to a curse. "It doesn't matter where you go. *You* belong everywhere, but you won't fit in anywhere. So, you might as well hang out with the misfits."

He spoke with deadpan conviction; he was not the best salesman. But maybe it was his gruffness, or the tilt of his head when he spoke, or the nervous wringing of his hand in his pocket, but for some reason I believed what he had to say.

"Is different funny?" I ask.

He laughed. "Different is just different. But world builders always want the whole world to change."

I explain to him that I just want to observe and be a witness.

"You should apply to my program. I don't believe you, I think you actually want to be in the game," he insists. "We are trying out something new next school year and I think you'd be the perfect fit. It's art for social change. Here you get to create your own shift."

"Excuse me?"

"That too..."

He presses me to consider his offer even though it is past the deadline, even though I was already accepted into a small university back home in Virginia, even though this school is someone else's wildest dream. I listen and nod my head yes. But inside my answer is, *yeah right, hell no.*

That man ended up being the head of the school and after answering a bunch of his questions, "What would you do if...?" "How do you feel about...?" he finally helped me see in myself what he saw in me clearly. "You're a creative. Not just a watcher. You're a maker. Nothing that exists will ever be enough for you, you'll always want to create."

As Marie and I drove back to Virginia, rolling past sprawling stretches of grass and nothingness, she goes on and on about the school having ceramics and glassblowing and writing and bookbinding and musical theater and sound design.

"People go to school for glassblowing?" I ask, half listening.

"Yes!" Marie exclaims.

That was twenty years ago, when my young and unstable life was shifting day by day. My parents were separating (again!), my mother, a former educator and librarian, was selling our house because she had completely lost her vision. She was moving back to her country in the Caribbean to listen to audiobooks in her hideaway. And meanwhile, my terminally ill dad was dying any day. Staying in Virginia was like staying enslaved to a story that I wasn't sure how to escape.

So I wrote an essay about meeting a gruffy man at the open

house and sent it to the admissions office of the University of the Arts writing program for social change. Marie made an accompanying movie for her own application to the film school.

"I wish people would shut up," I wrote as the first line to my essay. "And let their feet do the talking." I pitched the idea of a student-run club where we could sell and purchase each other's art and books and clothes, and the proceeds could be used to build community with Philly families who were our neighbors. I made it all up and laid it all out. It wasn't a fully developed bookshop back then, but my idea was always win/win/win.

A few weeks later, I got a large acceptance envelope in the mail with a presidential scholarship to the University of the Arts in Philadelphia, but my best friend Marie, who put all her eggs in one basket, got a small envelope with a rejection letter that read, "After careful consideration . . ."

I went to her house and consoled her and her mother's weeping eyes as we ate fried fish over rice. I reminded them that sometimes a no is the next best thing to a yes. But Maries are always a step ahead of you. When she finally stopped crying, Marie looked at me and said, "What if we move to Philly, anyway?"

After Marie and I had made several trips back and forth on our own, we started showing our mothers Philly. We went to City Hall (my favorite building, which happened to be a French revival–style castle with a courtyard where singers perform as you walk to the train). We took them past the still-in-progress Theatre of Life mural designed with thousands of shards of broken glass and hundreds of gallons of paint. We drove past *The Thinker* with his hand on his chin. We drove past Rocky's steps, even though I had never seen the film. But we all knew the hymn—dunadunnnnnnn duneunduuun. We tried to get them a cheese-oozing cheesesteak, but they both declined. We tried to give them every stereotypical Philadelphia experience that we could imagine. But as we approached the underground gallery mall, our mothers finally agreed, "Okay. Enough. Okay." We could move to Philly and experience her for ourselves.

Chapter 3

My parents, mostly caught up in the story of their own love affair, were confused by my sudden change of heart to move to Philly instead of staying in Virginia, but not enough to have anything significant to say. Neglect can be an ally; it just means fewer people to get in your way. Neither of my parents had gone to traditional college, only bible college, where they fell for one another over a love for holy books. In the seventies my mother got her first job as a librarian at a law firm in New York City. She got it as an immigrant without a degree, perhaps because she is very smart and very beautiful and very good at solving problems, maybe because she has a sweet accent and a complete and total love for books, but somehow, she became a law librarian for many years without any formal education.

Her philosophy with me was school or no school, you get your mission in life complete. All I told my parents was I was moving to Philadelphia. No one asked me much of anything. They gave me a $100 bill and said, "Okay." When they dropped me off in the city, they told me don't turn back, just keep running. In many ways, I felt like a runaway slave. I cried because I'd finally made it out of the South, then I dried my eyes, unpacked my pans, and made myself pancakes.

This was the beginning of my journey to the bookshops. I wish it included familiar book titles, and authors from the early nineties. But there are no cute stories about childhood visits to bookstores with my parents. They may have gone together, because they loved each other, but with me, that was just not the case. What they gave me were bible stories. Like Moses parting The Red Sea and Moses demanding freedom. "Let my people go!"

Those books are how I escaped.

Twenty years later and I'm still running toward the promised land. I'm still calling people for respite along the way. After several rings, my dad finally picks up the phone: "Hello."

"Lazarus, guess what?" I call my dad Lazarus because he has been terminally ill since I was ten years old. He almost dies every few years, priests and last rites, candles and all, but somehow he miraculously comes back to life like nothing happened. His dying is a joke, something to laugh about every time he wakes up.

"I'm gonna be a published author," I tell him. "I'm gonna sell my own books in my own bookshops. How cool is that?"

"It's about time, Number 2," he says. He doesn't call me by my first name, Jeannine; he calls me by my birth order. It works for my two sisters, number one and number three, just not for me. He thinks it's clever. I tell him it's not. It sounds like he's calling me poop. "Dad, you know what number two is, right?"

"Ah, shut up," he laughs.

I don't tell him about my diagnosis—I've kept it from him for fourteen years, no point in alarming him now. I don't tell him a lot of things, like how the bookshops are doing or how reading Chase-Riboud affects me or when I need a break. He does not want to hear poetic meanderings about me shedding my old self. My dad, like most people, just wants to hear about accomplishments and the next new shiny thing.

A Shopkeeper never complains.

"You're a young Tina Fey," my dad reminds me, ignoring my mood swings. "You're a young—well not so young—Tina Fey. Ain't she from Philly? You know you're not really from Philly, right?" My dad rapidly fires dad jokes when we speak. "You're from Brooklyn. Raised in VA. Don't forget where you came from, Number 2. You ain't never leaving Philly though, are you? You might as well run for governor you love it so much." He cracks himself up.

"Dad, Philly is not its own state."
I feel funny.
But I'll be okay.
He laughs and says, "Shut up, Jeannine."
I laugh and say ok.

Chapter 4

It's summer 2024 and I have just signed a two-book deal with HarperCollins. Three months to write an upmarket romance—the one genre of book that I just started to read. And three months to write a real raw memoir right after that.

My assignment this summer is to continue running multiple bookshops while telling the story of the bookshops. They say tell the story only you can tell. This is an Olympic-sized task.

My agent, my newest Marie (and eighty-plus-year-old best friend—the kind that tells me sternly what NOT to say), says I can do it and promises to hold my hand as we wade through the water. She's been in publishing longer than my parents have been alive. I am one of her many literary granddaughters.

"Just say YES," she tells me. "You have many stories inside."

I know they're in there, but some are stuffed so far down that I fear someone will have to cut them out to help them see the light of day.

The back of my dress is sun soaked with sweat as I think about writing my first novel. I am supposed to be writing about selling books to real people, but my editor at Amistad has a better idea—what if you write a series that takes place in a fictional bookshop universe?

"Like the X-Men of bookshops?" I ask.

It sounds genius, but I need a second opinion. So, I walk and talk on the phone with my dad. If I call him when I'm walking, he talks a lot, and it makes the walk go fast. He's not a good listener, but he is a great talker, which forces me to be a better listener. He used to be a falsetto singer in men's quartets, so when he gets hyped while he's speaking, he hits high notes that your brain cannot forget. I used to think it was his voice that tuned my inner ear to hear otherworldly frequencies. We've walked and talked like this off and on for the entire twenty years since I moved to Philly. Late nights, early mornings, it doesn't matter what's going on—when I call, he answers the phone.

Today I call to tell him I don't know how to write a book. All I know how to do is read them.

"I thought the bookshop was supposed to be a room of your own," my dad mimics me, mimicking Angelou, who was mimicking Woolf. "A place for you to read, write, and rest," he mocks.

"It is," I lie. "I write there sometimes," I lie again. The only thing I can do in the bookshops is fiddle and fidget and fix things.

*A Shopkeeper builds a sanctuary for others
until she learns how to build one for herself.*

So, I booked a ticket to Paris because not knowing the language makes it easier for me to hear. And not knowing the people makes it easier for me to see myself.

"You really think you're a lil' Baldwin type, don't you?" My dad hee-hees then haa-haas, then pauses, waiting for my comeback. "Probably drinking whiskey and smoking cigarettes now too," he continues. I stay quiet. Give him nothing. I don't feel like play arguing, sometimes he's my dad, and sometimes he's my big brother. "If you're looking for *your* history, you should come back down here to Virginia instead of going to Paris."

He fusses about me not knowing my own roots while chasing others'. "Come home and write about Jamestown and how chattel slavery was homegrown in your front yard. Come home and write about that. You worried about Josephine Baker when you should be worried about Ella Josephine Baker, who's from where you're from."

"That's not how it works, Dad."

I always think of my dad as a spy because he knows everything about everything and goes into the hospital all the time. He disappears for days or weeks and just comes back out of nowhere like he wasn't gone. I used to think "the hospital" was code for his secret missions.

Born in Brooklyn in the late fifties, he's lived in Hampton, Virginia, where I was raised, since the mid-nineties, but like almost all people born in Brooklyn, he always (always, always!) represents New York Knicks, Giants, Yankees.

Hampton was the home he wanted for his three daughters. He got trapped there and relaxed there and never left there, except the one time he moved in with me in Philly, but he moved right back to Hampton. He knows history, so he gives me research assignments that I don't want.

Like this:

"Look up Nellie Bright!" he says. "Bet you don't know a damn thing about no Nellie Bright." He speaks like a coach in the playoffs—forceful but with your best interest at heart. "Put Nellie Bright on one of your lil' bookshop tee shirts."

"Dad, why you gotta call my bookshop tee shirts little?" I ask with a chuckle and shaking of my head.

Lazarus is an armchair historian because instead of working, he's spent much of his life shackled to a bed or an armchair by IV tubes having his blood cleaned. He's a slave to maintaining his medical treatments, managing his sickness, being poked and prodded, and tolerating pain. He mostly sits still, watches sports, hangs with his friends, talks on the phone, and reads. He never complains about his condition. If anything, he's been spying on the medical industry this whole time and he knows all their secrets.

"Did you know you were raised in the first colony?"

"Yes, Dad," I tell him. "But. No, I can't write when I'm down there. And I don't want to write about colonization." Even as a kid I rebelled against field trips to plantations. "I want to write about what I like to read about—freedom. Rites of passage. Literary movement. Ascension. Think Baldwin, think Morrison, think Wright, Angelou, Joyce, Hemingway, Stein, think about the sanctity of Philly's own travelers—Franklin, Tanner, Robeson, Anderson, Holiday, Chase-Riboud, and Coltrane. And now . . . now I get to go on my own pilgrimage to visit the great mother of creativity in Paris, Isis."

"What?"

"Isis, Dad." I always have to tell him stuff again and again.

Sometimes my dad has no idea what I am talking about.

Isis is an ancient being who is believed to travel from time immemorial—she gathers pieces of the destroyed and puts them back together better than they were before. She is from before the ships, before the MAAFA, before the pyramids. She has wings. And gills and cow horns and a solar disk about her head. She is often depicted holding a baby. Some believe her spirit is strongest in Par(Is)is. Paris!

For some she is fact. For others she is fiction.

My dad still doesn't understand. He tells me I'm always going off on tangents, mixing history with mythology, that I never know the difference between what is real and what is fake. He is an awful listener. He changes the subject and speaks over me. I do it to him too, it's our way.

He tells me he just got a new prosthetic leg. Named it Lester. Says he and Lester would probably outrun me in the Olympics if I invite them to Paris, where the games will be held the summer while I am there. He has cheated death (again!) but lost his leg in the battle. We both laugh at Lester being the newest name on the family tree—and then I say right next to his name where my mother's name used to be. That's not funny he says. Jokes can go too far. I won't be inviting any of them on my trip, I remind him. I have too many distractions in my mind.

"Your doctor is making a killing off you," I say to Lazarus. "I bet he put all his children's children's children's children through medical school with your surgeries. Spleen, kidneys, liver, fingers, toes, a foot, and now a leg. It's kinda like what slaveowners would do if you were caught trying to escape. They would try to take a piece of your permanence away. If your doctors don't stop, eventually you will look like Mr. Potato Head."

He laughs. But I'm not joking.

"How's your mom?" His pitch shifts from high to low.

When he first met my mother in the early seventies she had just moved to this country from Trinidad and Tobago and he says it was love at first sight. He saw light shine from heaven when she walked into the church.

"She's fine, I guess." But the truth is I haven't spoken to her much lately. I'll write her her own memoir someday.

"I know she fine, that's why I married her," he hee hees.

I tell him I don't want to be in the middle of their situation. It makes me feel like Number 2.

Chapter 5

When I hang up, I realize that my dad is losing pieces of himself. He's disappearing like an apparition. I shouldn't just hang up on him.

At least he has Lester to keep him company, I think. I laugh out loud at my own joke. It's a funny bone joke. It aches. *At least he still has his funny bone.* I laugh out loud again. At least I am laughing. I call my condition absurd ambivalence—the ability to feel two opposing emotions at once without people noticing. I feel ok. I feel alright.

Chapter 6

I arrive a bit late to the bookshop and greet our youth conductors with a customer service smile. Youth conductors run the bookshops. It's an important part of our model. If I could, I would have them all trained by my mother like we've done in past summers—she's strict but loving and she reads constantly. Instead, they are being trained by me and having to work outside in the heat.

The conversations with Dr. Hahn and Lazarus have left a cramp in my side.

This summer the youth are selling used books outside of the bookshop on a table like I did throughout college.

When I was a student at the University of the Arts, in addition to taking an eclectic mix of art and education classes, I'd go outside of the school and set up books like *The Isis Papers* by Frances Cress Welsing and *Egyptian Mysteries* by Muata Ashby (books they didn't have in our art school library) alongside incense and oils and prints and clothes as I ran the student organization I envisioned in my admissions essay. I named the club Positive Minds—at eighteen years old, perhaps this was my first "bookshop."

We'd go book dumpster diving in the libraries of closing schools and find editions of old *Jet* and *Ebony* magazines. Other students would give us their misprints and deformed ceramic pots and abstract sculptures: whatever artwork they didn't want we got. People would bring us old books and old albums and all sorts of things. On the weekends me and my club members would take what we raised and all the media equipment we could check out and hit the streets to host events and share stories with the people we'd meet. My favorite part of being a story collector is you never know what life will bring. We hosted dinner and a movie series, where we watched a film that went with a book and got the food from a local business and invited the community to share our space. We hosted roundtable discussions and debates. We hosted maker sessions and just had folks come together to make.

I stayed on the Dean's List every year because I loved school even though I struggled at it. They sent me to tutoring for writing because when I was passionate, my professors weren't always sure of what I was trying to say. I would go visit the dean at the end of every semester to thank him for his support. He has written a few books and we are still friends today.

All these years, he has no idea I was living in a shell of a home back then. A shell of a home is basically just bricks and sticks—a building with a facade and a frame. I too felt like a shell of a home.

My dean had no idea I'd been throwing socks on a kerosene heater all winter to keep warm or that I was bathing with gallon jugs of water from the corner store. I was hiding from mice and crackheads, who both moved in and out of my "house" as they pleased. I was trying to remodel someone else's $1 house into a home, and it was not working for me.

I realize now that part of building the bookshops is me seeking to build a home for those who need one again and again.

In my last semester of college, two things happened.

One, I dropped out. I couldn't take it anymore. I was going back to Virginia to live with my dad. I was tired of begging to ride the city bus, not being able to shower, and pooping in a bag.

Freedom was coming at a cost that I could no longer afford.

I didn't know then what I know now. I am prone to seeing what's not there yet, running toward a vision with the force of an Olympian, keeping going no matter what, just closing my eyes and forging ahead until the next vision appears. Whenever I go too far off path, an angel whispers in my ear, then grips me by the shoulder, picks me up, and brings me back where I belong.

Jack Murnighan would not consider himself an angel. He's a rebellious, nerdy, New England genius bad-boy type with a doctorate in medieval literature, who writes about sex scenes in classic books from *Beowulf* to Dante's *Inferno*. He taught me reading and writing while sitting on an exercise ball.

The art school model had Jack as my professor for all four years at the University of the Arts, in six-hour studio classes like we were painters. We spent hundreds of hours together talking about writing and grammar and literature, and then I disappeared from school thinking no one would notice, because this is what happens, I get overwhelmed.

Jack happened to run into me at an art opening in North Philly, but I always joke that he was stalking me because why was he really hanging out in Norf? He said my classmates missed me asking one thousand questions and making our six-hour classes even longer by sharing my thoughts. He laughed and he gave me a book to read: *One Hundred Years of Solitude* by Gabriel García Márquez. He told me I could read this book over and over for the rest of my life and never catch everything. "Life is like a great book. It's okay to take your time, but you don't want to quit until you reach the end." A good story gets better with time.

Jack dropped me off at "home" and got to see the place in North Philly where I was living. He pretended not to be shocked or appalled or disgusted. Yes, it was a four-story 2,500-square-foot 1915 rowhome that retained its original Federal-style architectural integrity. That is what I loved about it. Yes, it was filled with revolutionary books by Kwame Nkrumah and Amiri Baraka and Frantz Fanon and Malcolm X's autobiography and articles by Marcus Garvey, tons of articles, DVDs, and papers about ancient Kemet and the flower of life and how-to books on just about everything, art supplies for screen printing and airbrushing, and a hall mural of twelve-foot sphinxes, but my home hardly had any walls, no bathroom, no kitchen, no stove, no sink, no anything. I was learning to drywall and lay floors and installing installation instead of learning glassblowing and bookbinding, so I would have a warm place to lay my head and a literal pot to piss in. It was unbalanced.

Jack said, even though I had fallen on tough times, I could still finish school. I tried to explain that I hadn't fallen on tough times, I had a vision for this space. But he told me to consider finishing my degree just in case so that one day if I needed it, I could get a regular job.

Jack said all I had to do was take four independent studies to graduate. Each one could be a class of my choosing with a syllabus that I got to create. I could choose any mentors who would sign off on my work in their "classes." He said, "It's art school. You finish in your own way."

I said, "Okay."

So I chose what I call "Jeannine's Angels": David Brown, my professor of social advertising, who introduced me to how to build a campaign (*Hey Whipple, Squeeze This*); Toby Zinman, a renowned literary critic (she made me read a novel a week and a play a day—she introduced me to Morrison and Wilson and Parks and Dickinson and Mamet and Dostoevsky); Slavko Milekić, a cognitive scientist (introduced me to *Touching* by Ashley Montagu, and *To Touch is to Live* and a world where art was science-based); and Jack Murnighan, who knew my housing situation but never told a soul. He gifted me his entire book collection, some of which looked a thousand years old. His collection introduced me to almost everything.

Finally, Sara MacDonald was my school librarian and although she wasn't my advisor, she was also an angel. She let me practically live in the basement of the school library, take naps down there, sit alone, stare and think.

I would say it was my angels who taught me how to read, read.

I believe we all have literary angels. People who guide the direction of our lives through the books they share with us. It's a tradition passed down for ages. Twenty years later, Jack, Toby, Slavko, David, Sara, the director and the dean, are still angels in my life to different degrees. They still recommend books to me. I call my angels when I find out that after almost 150 years of cultivating creatives, it is announced that the University of the Arts abruptly closed its doors for good. This news shatters the entire city and thousands of students. How does one grieve an institution?

By passing down the tradition to the next generation in other ways.

Our current used book collection at Harriett's was gifted to the youth conductors by Barbara Schmidt-Vance, the daughter of a local judge—Harvey Schmidt, who has passed away. In 1965 he started the first ever Community Legal Services clinic in Philadelphia. He provided free and low-cost legal support for communities who couldn't afford it any other way. One of the youth, Elizah, is holding a first edition copy of *Black's Law Dictionary* in his hands and I'm not sure he knows what that means.

Books are for time travel, I tell the youth, they help us to find freedom; we don't need to invent a way out, when the way has already been made. All we have to do is shut up and read. I point at a few crooked stacks about government, language, and space. The youth straighten the books and say, "Okay."

I ask them what they're liking in the collection, to make sure they are reading from it and not just playing around in it. For some reason this cohort has gravitated to *All About Love* by bell hooks, maybe because she's recently passed away.

I tell them about the time I was in France and I met two bell hooks scholars who had fallen in love while caring for her. We were supposed to be in a conference but instead they let me be their third wheel for the day. We ditched the conference to meditate in a church designed by Matisse for a nun whom he loved. They didn't need to tell me anything; they let me feel the vibration of their love. I ask the youth what love sounds like; they look at me puzzled and try to understand what I mean. Not how it feels, not what it looks like, but how does it sound? After a short debate, they agree they can't explain.

Love sounds like silence, I tell them. Listen to her, she's calling your names.

Some laugh and some customer service smile. They think I am being funny when I'm being serious and serious when I'm being funny. I smile and walk away.

Chapter 7

I look up at the front of our four-story, brick-front building before walking in. After five years of strongly suggesting and then damn near begging my landlord to sell me this building, she has finally agreed. In a few weeks, it will be ours. That's if things go as planned, but when do things ever go as planned?

When I get inside the shop, I check for the prescription in my pocket and promise to run across the street to Nova Star pharmacy to fill it before the end of the day. I am thankful for Mrs. Graves—an awful name for a beautiful disease that has not taken my spleen, kidneys, fingers, legs, or toes away. Mrs. Graves just fuels my fire. She drives me, but sometimes she drives me insane. I keep the graveness of Mrs. Graves to myself and just use the fuel to haul boxes of paperbacks of *The 1619 Project* from the front of the shop into the back. I am at Harriett's, getting ready to head to our sister bookshop, Ida's.

I should be rereading *The 1619 Project* by Nikole Hannah-Jones, who we will be hosting at our sister bookshop in South Jersey in just a few days. I am not the fastest reader. Which is why I question why I volunteered for this assignment. So many people seem far better equipped than me. I have to read things over and over again to process them. I can't remember titles or names. One paragraph can leave me spiraling for days, "What did she mean by that?" One line in one poem can take my breath away.

I am the organizer and interviewer for the book talk at Ida's. The two jobs are not the same. One side of my brain knows the books need to be counted, inventoried, and stacked so they are ready for transport and display. And then the other side will reread and reread, like a nervous tic, so I am overprepared for the conversation with Nikole Hannah-Jones for what we're calling our "Happy Birthday, Ida" event. I am interested in how a single book can be the impetus for measurable social change. How reading together as a community to address a single issue in a deep way could work for more than a single book event. I am trying this idea out in South Jersey. I am also midway through my ever-increasing lease and I have to decide if I want to stay or leave. Rising rent is the silent bookshop killer.

Our sister shop, Ida's Bookshop, opened in 2021, one year after Harriett's, because I visited a small suburban county in South Jersey looking for used furniture and I met a guy who was a city commissioner selling midcentury modern couches. He mentioned to the mayor that I was in town and the mayor called me and said if I ever wanted to open a sister bookshop on their main street, they'd move mountains to have me there. Right away I knew the name for our next shop: Ida's Bookshop, named for investigative reporter and journalist Ida B. Wells. For months I traveled in Ms. Ida's footsteps while reading her incomplete autobiography, *A Sword Among Lions*. I visited the home in Holly Springs, Mississippi, where she was born a slave. I walked through the house, and became acquainted with her. I got stuck in Mississippi because there were no Ubers or taxis there and thought it was a great metaphor—of how hard it must have been for Ida to escape from there.

Then I visited the part of Memphis where she ran a newspaper whose office got burned to the ground. There's a plaque there in her name, but I ask myself, what does a plaque change? I visited the street where her friends were lynched, left flowers in their memory, then I went to Chicago to see the home she made for her family. After walking and listening to her for some time, I opened Ida's Bookshop at 734 Haddon Avenue in Collingswood, New Jersey, in her name.

Come to find out, Ms. Ida is also Nikole Hannah-Jones's matron saint. She also walks and talks with her. She is coming to celebrate with us on the birthday of the bookshop for an event that coincides with the actual birthday of Ida B. Wells.

I dream of a weekend-long book event where all fifty of *The 1619 Project*'s contributors, from Sonia Sanchez to Tiya Miles to Jesmyn Ward, share one stage and sign all the books together, but who can pull that off? Not me. Not yet anyway.

Even without my big idea, over eight hundred people from South Jersey (where I have to beg publishers to send authors) have registered for our "birthday event." Only about forty of them can fit inside our bookshop, so I have to figure out a solution, quick!

A Shopkeeper tells the folks who say books are dead to shut up and read.

I should be starting to write my novel, but who can write a book when you have eight hundred people coming to visit? I am doing the job of my three young summer interns. But they look so happy selling used copies of *In the Matter of Color* and *The Philadelphia Negro* from Judge Schmidt's collection that I tell them they can go get water ice on me during their break. It's summertime in Will Smith's Philadelphia and they're just kids.

Chapter 8

Harriett's was my last resort.

I opened Harriett's Bookshop, named for historic heroine Harriett Tubman, six weeks before the pandemic, and could have never predicted that my tiny shop would survive and thrive—being featured in *Oprah Magazine, Vogue, Forbes, The New York Times, Inc., Essence, The Washington Post*, Google, the *Today* show, Yahoo, NPR, MSNBC, ABC, and CBS for our out-of-the-box approaches to sharing books. Or that, in just a few years, we'd expand our network of sister bookshops from Philadelphia to Paris and that I'd be responsible for hosting authors like Michelle Obama, Will Smith, Kerry Washington, Salamishah Tillet, Lorene Cary, Alice Walker, Sonia Sanchez, Sister Souljah, and Nikki Giovanni, just to name a few. Or most importantly, all the everyday people, places, and things (jawns as a Philadelphian might say) that Harriett's would someday touch. The only issue was I opened Harriett's because I needed a quiet place to write. And then I lost track of my mission, so everyone else had a place to read.

According to my landlord, our Fishtown storefront had been a nail salon, a café, and most recently a cell phone repair spot. It was painted a decrepit shade of lavender-ish gray and had peeling rubber trim and a giant hole in the floor. I called it a portal, painted it with my uncle, and threw some putty and a rug over the hole. It was like playing make pretend. Sometimes a healthy imagination is helpful. Now, five years later, this building will be a home for Harriett's.

On February 1, 2020, I opened Harriett's to celebrate women authors, artists, and activists. Americans typically learn about Harriett Tubman in the third grade—that she ran the underground railroad and freed the enslaved. But to me she has always been more than a historic figure or a slave: Harriett is my guide, and following her footsteps makes me feel brave. Like Harriett, my first stop toward freedom was Philadelphia, where the story of my bookshops begins.

At our opening in the Fishtown section of Philadelphia, people from all walks of life showed up in droves to purchase what books we had. My sister stayed up all night to talk me through fits of anxiety, Marie was there early checking out readers from 6 a.m. to 6 p.m., my aunt drove up from North Carolina to give me her journal to read.

But six weeks later, midday in mid-March of 2020, we received an email from the mayor that read—"effective immediately"— shut the doors to your cute little bookshop and don't open them again. Then there was a deadly COVID-19 outbreak, and my mother, who was living in Trinidad, got stuck at my place in Philadelphia on a visit, and then heat waves, and my sister got married, and #MeToo, a racial uprising, vaccines, anti-vaccines, the contested election, wildfires, a war, and even Ruth Bader Ginsburg died—2020 was that type of year.

But here we are a few years later, and Harriett's, a small independent bookshop, survived all of that.

A Shopkeeper should do the job that ONLY she can do, let others take care of the rest. Easier said than done.

We survived to serve hundreds of thousands of people worldwide. We survived to build bookshops in unconventional places from movie theaters to barns. We survived so we could distribute literature in our city and then to organizers at protests from Minneapolis to Louisville. We survived to get Harriett Tubman Day passed by Congress as the first federal holiday named for a woman. We survived so we could deliver books to children on horseback. We survived so I could write this book.

Who would have imagined that in less than five years, we'd have books and multiple bookshop concepts across the globe named for women in history?

When I first met my landlord, Ms. Sang, I told her, "I want to open a bookshop here."

"A bookshop?" She scrunched up her forehead in dismay. "In Fishtown?" She shook her head no.

"Yeah, a creative space celebrating women authors, artists, and activists under the guiding light of Harriett Tubman."

"Harriett who?"

"Tubman."

"I don't know her. But I see something in you," my landlord said, looking me in my eyes the way people look at me sometimes, with a peculiar, puzzled pause. "But, if you meet Oprah Winfrey, I want to be there."

"Oprah?" I laughed. Not what I expected.

"I'll make a deal with you," she said, pointing at me uncomfortably close. "You get the lease to this storefront if you promise to introduce me to Oprah someday."

I didn't know how I could ever meet Oprah, or how that could be a priority when I didn't know how I was going to pay my next month's rent.

But I said, "Okay. You have a deal."

We shook on it.

Five years later, the bookshop has been featured by Oprah's magazine twice for being one of 2,433 independent bookstores in the country that still exist. This number has steadily decreased in the last few years and, in our own ways, we are each at risk.

Ms. Sang calls me and says, "I saw you on the news." Out of the blue she tells me she is tired and ready to sell her building to me. "There's no one who will love this place like you." I felt like I'd passed a test even though she hadn't met Oprah yet, then she added, "But I still want to meet Oprah."

I do love the building, except for the plumbing and HVAC that need to be replaced.

I want to finish the remodel and close on the sale—another Olympic-sized task for an average-sized Jeannine, but to whom much is given . . .

A Shopkeeper knows she has to own her own building if she wants to sustain. Rent is the silent bookshop killer because it never stops beating you up even when you're down.

I have recently been given the Philadelphia Cultural Treasures award. But it's Harriett's that is the cultural treasure, not me. I am using the award to reimagine the bookshop, because every few months I redesign it to promote a different book and theme in my community. I am also going on a pilgrimage to Paris to write my debut novel.

Chapter 9

As I walk into Harriett's, John and his team of contractors are starting to build our new bar and shelves. I can finally make this space my own, now that I own it—well, almost own it. It's so close I can smell it. I can also smell that someone has been smoking cigarettes inside here, despite me repeatedly asking them not to; they put it out before I can figure out who. We are transforming our 500-square-foot space into a café with a rotating menu of drinks, bites, and books customized to the theme we are sharing. It's like a full immersion that integrates local chefs and mixologists and authors and musicians.

We are starting with *The Age of Phillis* by Honorée Fanonne Jeffers. I write Honorée and tell her some of my plans. Since completing her book she's received every type of award. We have a digital ki-ki about her greatness and the exhibit I am building called Phillis' Librarie. Our menu is based on items that were exported on ships from West Africa alongside one of the most storied published poets in United States history, Phillis Wheatley, who published her *Poems on Various Subjects, Religious and Moral* in 1773. Through the experience visitors receive copies of the book, they ride a trolley while writing poetry to Phillis' spirit, they visit a local tea shop that has prepared a specialized tea drink in Phillis' honor, they record their poem in a podcast studio, they ride pass the park that used to be named for her, they tour an art exhibit in her name accompanied by a young lady on violin, and then they get a tour of the African American Museum in Philadelphia all in one day.

While Wheatley never lived in Philadelphia, in 1922 there was a citywide campaign to honor a South Philly park (which just happens to be my neighborhood park) in her name. At the turn of the century, this name sparked massive upheaval among residents, and ultimately the name was changed to honor someone else. I believe Ms. Phillis still deserves her own space in Philadelphia history, but right now her exhibit in my place smells like sweaty men, cigarette smoke, and demolition.

I want a secret door, I tell John, pointing at the perfect place in the wall that would lead to the Underground—what we call the bookshop basement that floods at least once a year, but otherwise is a cool underground space. He gives me a thumbs-up. The AC isn't working so it's twice as hot inside as it is outside, but it's always cooler in the Underground.

Contractors are climbing over each other to meet my impossible constant demand of reopening before I leave for Paris. It's loud and noisy and dusty and buzzing with too many voices and too much energy. It's like my mind reflected outside of me.

A Shopkeeper knows that bookshops that only sell books can barely sustain themselves anymore—that's why now we all sell mugs and tee shirts and socks and soaps and candles and coffees and teas and plants and clothes and if you're lucky—alcohol. A Shopkeeper prefers books.

I sit down in a corner to read through a stack of galleys when a woman rushes in, crying and shaking her hands at me. "Welcome to Harriett's." I stand up to greet her. "How may I help you, my friend?" She says she just saw her biological father out front. She can't find the words to explain. She's hyperventilating. Her father doesn't want a relationship with her and she's heartbroken. My contractors continue hammering as my customer sobs into my hot sticky chest. I pat her back and say nothing. My mother is much better at these moments. She's warm and tender. It's probably what made her a great librarian. She is sensitive. But me, I am thinking of what title to suggest—*Sweet Summer* by Bebe Moore Campbell comes to mind like a remedy for abandonment. Or what action she can take, like start a support group in our bookshop basement.

When she stops crying, she apologizes. I tell her no need. This is what bookshops are for. She agrees. When I don't know what to say, I just listen. The woman tells me she is going to miss the old bookshop design. She points at the black-and-white wallpaper that the contractors are tearing down. But that old design is out of here. She promises to buy a book next time and leaves.

Chapter 10

A Shopkeeper knows her limits.

I am supposed to run across the street to get my prescription. But I keep forgetting. I decide maybe Mrs. Graves is here to serve me. Perhaps it is she who helps me to hear more deeply from people beyond the grave, women like Harriett Tubman and Ida B. Wells and Josephine Baker. Maybe sitting with Mrs. Graves is like sitting in a graveyard, so close to death that it gives me a sixth sense. I sit down in the corner to breathe.

Breathe in Lorene Cary. I'm reading her memoir *Ladysitting* (again!) to prepare for a big book festival interview with her in the fall. Her memoir is about her last year with her nana. It grapples with the highs and lows of death, dying, caretaking, and pain while also being an activist in the community where she's built one of the largest and most impactful arts and culture organizations to date. The Art Sanctuary.

Lorene is my Philly Tainty. A Caribbean word for Auntie. We have shared West Indian roots and a shared love for Harriett. She's also a super smart historian and cultural preservationist and she's written a ton of books. So, I adopted her. And asked her to be my literary aunt. She was producing *My General Tubman* when I first opened Harriett's five years ago. I wrote her a cold email and asked if she'd be the first author to read at our bookshop. She agreed to come launch her memoir, *Ladysitting*, with us and then to tell stories about Harriett Tubman for the rest of the evening. Five years later, *Ladysitting* is being made into a play. This woman's genius is fascinating. Women like her are the reason why our mission celebrates women authors, artists, and activists, because they are amazing! Mindboggling = Lorene.

Poems . . . check.
Plays . . . check.
Memoirs . . . check.
Novels . . . check.
Vote That Jawn . . . check.
School board . . . check.
Tenured professor . . . check.
Art Sanctuary . . . check.
The Celebration of Black Writing . . . check.

I ask her if I can get a mural of her made on the front of our building and she's like, "Jeez, Jeannine."

Lorene makes me smile and reminds me the literary tradition is alive.

She lets me do communications for her organization, to make money when book sales are slow. She explains to me about publishing and how editing is supposed to go. She says to me once that her husband says to her, "Jeannine is your Lorene."

Pause out the electric bill and the gas. Silence the water bill and the insurance. Book bills are stacking up. Oh, don't I know it. Reading Lorene's work slows my heartbeat, stills my mind. I read single passages over and over because her passages remind me to breathe and slow down.

One day, Lorene and I agree to have a tea at Talula's Garden outside of the park at Lincoln Square in South Philly. It drizzles as we sip under an awning. She in a rain jacket and me in my furry peacoat. She calls me *shuggs* as she tells me about a Haitian chef who was French trained and came to Philadelphia enslaved, but his food was so exceptional that when he escaped, they tried to track him down by the taste.

I tell her the story of a recent trip I had:

"So the other day I met a woman, her name is Madi, who is a director, and we decide we're gonna go to New York City to see Philly's own James Ijames's show, *Fat Ham*, on Broadway. We get front-row seats. We spend the day getting to know one another eating together and talking, it's fun. After the show we get a call from Madi's sister who has just watched an opera that is making her weep into the phone. 'Where are you?' Madi asks her sister. Her sister is in Tennessee. I'm trying to stay out of their business, but Madi introduces me to her sister. Her sister suddenly stops crying and says, you two have to come and see this show. And I'm thinking I don't even know these people; her sister explains the opera is only two nights and tomorrow is the last show. It's being produced by this composer by the name of Hannibal who used to be the guest composer for the Philadelphia Orchestra. She says Hannibal is her neighbor and friend and that he has composed an opera about the middle passage and the Haitian Revolution and Jazz and the Blues and orishas and it's everything. She says, I'll buy your tickets to Tennessee and your tickets to the opera, but I need you to come have this experience. So even though I've just met this woman Madi, and never met her sister, now we're flying on a plane together to Tennessee to see an opera. The whole way there I kept singing to Madi the song 'Tennessee' by Arrested Development. 'Take me to another place, Take me to another land. Make me forget all that hurts me. Let me understand your plan.'

"Then I got into the music hall and I met the most majestic being, Hannibal Lokumbe, who was giving a talk on his piece, which includes over 300 performers. The entire stage was a constantly transforming ship. He said don't be afraid to yell out if you feel something. I cried and weeped and yelled out so bad in that theater that they asked me if I needed to be seen by someone, as the mothers from the hull moaned in agony at giving birth in chains while on slave ship while leaving their land, a choir sings, a 100-piece orchestra plays in the pit of a stage they've built just for these two nights. I've never felt something so beautiful, yet so disturbing. Ambivalence. Hannibal says he was called into the forest to write and compose music for instruments that he'd never played. He said he stayed outside in the woods for weeks until his nose began to bleed. When it was all over, I was sitting in the corner trying to avoid the crowd, because you know how I can be, when the singer, Kamaal, from Arrested Development, comes up singing 'Tennessee' behind me. He's seen the show. Madi and her sister can't believe it; I've been singing it all day. Before I realize what is happening, I turn around and Hannibal is standing beside me telling me that if I want to write, I need to listen to 'A Love Supreme' and he starts cracking up, singing it on repeat—'A Love Supreme, A Love Supreme.' I got back to Philly and felt like my life is a fever dream."

I'm going on and on when Lorene starts laughing.

I think it's funny too.

She looks me in the eye and finally says, "Yes, I was there in Tennessee at that show too."

"Tennessee."

I am like no way, she says yes, Hannibal is her good friend. "I write about him in *Ladysitting*!"

"No way? That's the same composer who your nana loved on the trumpet?"

"That's him."

"Shut the front door."

"Indeed. We always end up sitting next to who we are supposed to, now don't we."

"Indeed."

Chapter 11

Dear Ms. Harriett—

I am concerned about your bookshop, and all bookshops. Last year A VERY BIG COMPANY sold $28 billion worth of books. Who is still buying books from A VERY BIG COMPANY, you ask? The answer is clear, it's everyone. THAT VERY BIG COMPANY may make more money off this book that I am writing than me. I spent almost my entire book advance paying off book distributors to keep the bookshop open another year. The margins are thin. AI is alive. And if you can't book a celebrity author then it's THE END. Game over. Finito. Goodbye. I purchased 500 copies of *Ladysitting* and decided I will just sell those until I die. It's win/win/win. It helps Lorene. It helps Philly. It helps Harriett's. I hope this works. But one of my mentors says I need to add coffee and tea and desserts. I've never sold anything but books. He says I must think about the bottom line. But I'm just thinking about you. Thank you for thinking of me too.

                                Much love,
                                Jeannine

Chapter 12

This is NOT what I am supposed to be writing—love letters to my imaginary friends—but at least I've written something more than I wrote yesterday. I am 50,000 words away from a novel and having a book of my own like all the people I admire whose books I sell. I wish I were like Murakami with his disciplined schedule and strict routine self, or like Morrison at the crack of dawn with a yellow notepad, or like Laties, who must be psychic because as I was reading his book, *Rebel Bookseller*, he sends me a message encouraging me not to give up. I had never even met him before. I shut up and read.

Today, instead of selling books or writing the novel that I am commissioned to write, I am renovating my bookshop (again!). I am a bit obsessed with building a home for Harriett's.

"Which color?" John, my quasi-spiritual quasi-quack contractor, interrupts my daydreaming and self-analysis, holding up eight shades of blue paint.

Originally, I wanted blue walls because I thought my throat chakra was clogged from all the things I have not said. But with all the blues in front of me, I realize I have spoken to almost every major news outlet and every other podcaster, blogger, and influencer who has sent me a request. I've said a lot for a quiet introvert. I hope it helps.

Then I thought blue represented the waters that Wheatley

sailed on as she crossed the Middle Passage on a ship named *Phillis*. Or maybe blue was for Yemaya who protected Phillis the child writing prodigy. little seven-year-old head. Or the Mami Wata, who swam beside her on her journey. My fingers hover over each shade—sky blue, turquoise blue, seafoam blue, cerulean.

My trembling finger settles over a deep indigo. It's the color of the head above your head, John tells me. It's the color of wisdom, intuition, instinct, and understanding, the color of my great-grandmother's fingertips on a South Carolina indigo field, I tell John. He hands me the swatch to hold.

"The crown chakra connects us to something higher than ourselves. This blue calls you to stop speaking so much, sit still—listen, instead—this blue is meant to connect you with a realm that perhaps you can't see, but he that hath an ear, let them hear."

And I thought John was just here to do construction. I thank him and tell him enough. That's the new color for Harriett's.

Indigo.

Next, we paint.

A Shopkeeper remembers everything is unfolding in perfect order.

Chapter 13

As John is leaving to get tools, he promises to come back that evening to clean up and stay until the walls and floors are finished.

"When you walk in tomorrow, this place will be brand new," he vows.

As he leaves, my makeup artist, Tifah, arrives with her bamboo earrings swinging loud, extra-large braids plaited down her back, and an early nineties tracksuit that makes swishing sounds.

"You don't look ready," she says.

"Ready for what?"

"Your award."

I forgot about the award, even though she's reminded me twice. I am covered in a layer of dust. I share with her that I don't want to attend the ceremony. Crowds make my heart feel like I've been in a fight. Winning would be worse, especially if I have to give a speech. Speeches put acidic chalk in my mouth and electronic butterflies in my belly.

"But you do it so well," Tifah insists. "For the people. No matter how nervous you get, you always get it done for the people. It's like a switch. Just turn it on."

I am nominated for Entrepreneur of the Year by the Philadelphia Citizen. Stopping work to be awarded for work never makes sense to me. But it would be rude not to show. If I do all of this and not win, I'm gonna be so pissed at Tifah. I thought I had the night to myself.

"Just go wash up in the bathroom," she tells me. "I'll do something to your face." She's sure there's a dress in the basement I can wear. I do as I am instructed. Scrub my hands, underarms, and chest with stacks and stacks of soapy paper towels until I smell like Dr. Bronner's lavender soap, then I air dry, which feels refreshing against the Philly in July heat.

Taking time for makeup makes me sit still. Calm down. Reflect. Take it all in.

Breathe in Lorene writing, "the certain way to ease anxiety is love."

Breathe out germs and phobias and overwhelm.

In the storage room Tifah finds me a pink pants suit—it's probably my mother's—and she decides to color my eyelashes and eyelids pink to match. I would have never chosen pink. It makes me feel too fragile, too soft and too melty like cotton candy. Tifah begins taking care of me, massaging my temples and applying my warrior paint. She likes the pink.

"It's unsuspecting," she says.

I feel her warm breath on my forehead as she paints me a new face. She is like a mother to me. She is like a sister. Tifah is dressing me up like Shug did Celie in *The Color Purple*, so we listen to the Quincy Jones soundtrack—"Miss Celie's Blues." She brushes away the dark spots under my eyes and the blotches around my chin. She plucks the overgrown hairs from my upper lip and the whiskers from my cheeks. She adds blush to make me look more alive and gloss to make me look hydrated. You need more sleep, and more water, she reminds me. I nod my head yes.

"What will you say when you win?" she asks.

"You mean IF I win."
"I mean WHEN you win!"
"I'll tell a story."

A Shopkeeper knows that a good story eases the mind.

"Tell the story about that time you started riding on horseback to deliver books to kids."

"Okay," I say.

"People love that story of you being taught to ride by the eighty-year-old man from Fletcher Street Riding Club and how you went around during COVID delivering free books to kids on horseback."

I just thought it would be a fun way to stay six feet apart from children while making sure they had books when they needed them.

"Or tell the story of opening six weeks before COVID and putting books outside for folks to grab on an honor system."

"Okay," I say, but that's not the right story either. We'd build the bookshop outside every day with a sign that said "Take one." Then someone sent that to Oprah and then came Stephanie Ruhle and MSNBC and next thing you know I had a six-part series about staying open during COVID and I was teaching them—the answer is always community.

I'll tell the origin story—how on my thirty-sixth birthday, November 28, 2019, I decided to open a bookshop under the guiding light of Harriett Tubman. Americans typically learn about Harriett in the third grade—that she ran the underground railroad and freed the enslaved. But I knew her, knew her. I knew her from stories that she embodied the creative spirit. Anyone who could be a spy, a nurse, a bricklayer, a general, a lover, a medicine woman, and a friend in one lifetime had to be possessed by the spirit of creativity. So, I started writing to her in my journal, *Conversations with Harriett*, asking her HOW? How she became a wade-through-waist-high-water-in-the-winter type of woman and if she could do it—how could I?

A bookshop, we both agreed.

Up until my thirty-sixth birthday, I thought opening a bookshop was something I'd do in my old age. Like anyone raised by a blind former librarian, former seminarian, I thought of course I'll be a book lady someday. But as it turned out, I was more a boho artsy type, working three jobs at a time and having never owned anything, except the $150,000 in student loan debt that I racked up getting art degree after art degree after art degree because I was possessed by the creative spirit too.

And as if I didn't have enough on my plate, a few months before my birthday, I decided to help an old flame, "the man," who quickly became more than an old flame once again. The only reason I met "the man" was because he was out in front of his North Philly rowhome selling, you guessed it, books.

But now the man was reinventing himself into a young politician. I know I should have known better. But this time around, I thought, what if this work changes him? I felt he was a North Philly Mandela deep down inside. But quite quickly I found out he was no Madiba. And I, no Winnie.

I could not stand behind this guy who was suddenly wearing sunglasses and trucker hats and coming home drunk every night. I kept saying to myself this can't be *love*, this can't be my legacy, no matter how handsome he may be and how big his muscles might get, no matter how much I *love* him, I could not hide behind him. I could not go down in the story of my life like that.

By the eve of his big event, I'd enlisted everyone and their mama literally to help "the man."

Then as usual "the man" came home at 2 a.m. stinking, stumbling drunk. That night, I think he sensed that I had had enough. He came in quickly, took off his campaign tee shirt and put on nothing but a navy blue towel.

"You stink," I said.

"What did you say?"

"You stink and I'm leaving," I said finally, brave enough to say it out loud. I brushed past him to leave the room. He followed me to the kitchen.

And then he responded without words and instead grabbed me by the back of my hair and threw me down on the hardwood kitchen floor.

The fact that I was feeding a small army, while he was out getting white-boy-wasted.

The fact that I was working three other jobs to make ends meet.

All of this exploded that night. And it ended up with him butt-ass naked (because in his rage he lost that navy blue towel). He was spitting and cursing—it felt like I was fighting with a rabid-ass dog. I thought of the dog in one of my favorite books, *The Pilgrimage* by Paulo Coehlo. In the story a dog continues to follow Paulo along his journey on the road to Santiago. Every time the dog appears it takes on a new persona; sometimes it is jovial and friendly, sometimes it is sick and needy, but no matter what persona it takes, by the end of the scene the dog switches and tries to kill Paulo. Paulo explains that we all have a dog that reappears on our journey over and over again in different forms, but our work is how to defeat it once and for all and not going back to play with it. When I flash back to reality, my eyes are wide and teary, my pregnant best friend, Marie, is screaming for "the man" to stop while he mops the floor with my face.

I started my Drexel University MFA writing program the next day bruised and scratched and bitten. I wore a cool outfit though—bleached baggy jeans, a graphic tee I designed that said "Zora, Octavia, Alice, Toni" in honor of my literary foremothers—and sunglasses for obvious reasons. I didn't want to go to Drexel (or anywhere that day)—my wrist ached, my ribs ached, I had a limp—but I'm glad Marie made me go and drove me and said prayers over me.

I started at Drexel to learn about story structure and narrative. But what I really wanted to learn was how to write a new story for myself. Strangely enough on that first day, when I could barely breathe let alone pay attention, the director of the program asked us who would guide us through to the end of the journey and I declared to the group it would be Toni Morrison, but in the back of my head I was thinking *Harriett Tubman and Ida B. Wells and Josephine Baker and my grandmothers and all those who came before me. They all have the same spirit.*

That's when I decided I was gonna find my way out of the wilderness, like Harriett in the freezing cold with a bounty on her head and dogs on her back. I looked at Marie and said, "Let's get the fuck outta here."

And we did.

We packed clothes in trash bags, scooped up books and journals, grabbed some snacks and ran away from my plantation. We ran from Philly back to our childhood home in Virginia.

Marie's mom said she would rent us a house when we got to Virginia. All would be well, I'd finish school online, but when we got down there it was a whole other story. Marie's mom meant well, but she didn't actually have the means to get us a place to live. We had escaped, but this wasn't freedom.

I kept asking for a sign.

The next day got harder with us trying to find a place, looking for jobs, and getting food. One of my friends offered us a beautiful three-story Airbnb to stay in in Norfolk, Virginia, a small beach town on the Chesapeake Bay, while I tried to make sense of things.

Before we ate, I walked to the beach to think and instead, I saw four dolphins. I was raised in this area, we went to this beach all the time when we were children, but I'd never once seen dolphins. Yet there they were, dancing in the distance on the ocean right in front of me.

Here was the sign I needed. I just knew it was one. Because come on, dolphins in December? Harriett was obsessed with dolphins. She was rumored to have said they carried messages from our ancestors who jumped ship during the Middle Passage.

While I was on the beach, my shamanic friend from Maryland called. She lived on Maryland's Eastern Shore, where Harriett was born and raised. I told her about my escape from Virginia to Philly and now back to Virginia and she asked, "What are you escaping from?"

I couldn't answer. But I thought perhaps it was a version of my story that I just couldn't take.

She said the dolphins represented the Mami Wata, meaning the grandmothers of the water. The Mami Wata are water deities associated with good fortune. They often look like mermaids, women with fishtails who can be beneficent or malevolent depending on the obedience of their followers. And that's when it came to me.

I have a house, I have a building, I have skills, I have degrees, I am a whole person. I'm going back to Philly, where I've built my life and my community. Like Harriett, I would heed the call and head back. Ms. Harriett would agree it's okay to go back and forth again and again to re-free yourself.

Tifah hands me a cracked mirror to break me out of my storytelling daydream and bring me back to reality.

"You're beautiful," she says about my cracked face.

The crack is so deep, I can't see what she sees. But I trust her.

"Ain't no stopping us now, we're on the move," she hums as I slip into someone else's pink suit. She sprays me with something sweet smelling. Now I smell like someone else's perfume. I run down into the basement and come back up to give Tifah a stack of children's books about dinosaurs for her sons.

Then we duck and dodge through downtown traffic. I arrive at the Kimpton Hotel for the award ceremony and sit in a back corner of the moody bar instead of going upstairs to the event. I order a glass of crisp whiskey and water. I say cheers to myself in the mirror. Congrats. Here's your reward for showing up for life even when you really don't want to.

I time it so I am not standing around doing nothing.

8:05 p.m.

For five minutes I review the renovation plan—floors, paint, and hardware. Realize John is three days behind schedule. Three days!

8:10 p.m.

Five minutes to review my itinerary to Paris—airline, lodging, and transportation. Try to see if I can push back my dates. I cannot.

8:20 p.m.

Ten minutes to highlight sections of *The 1619 Project*, as political pundits argue that it is this book, and not history, that's causing the growing tension that has ravaged the small South Jersey town where Ida's Bookshop lives.

8:30 p.m.

And then ten minutes of silent observation. I settle into the coziness of my quiet corner with my pen. A hot young couple sits across from each other heads down, not speaking. They are both on their phones. A single gentleman drinking a martini sits next to a single woman drinking a martini—yet neither notices the other. They are both on their phones. The tall bartender, the sexy hostess, the muscular waiter—phone, phone, phone. The bar is quiet except for the elevator music that plays too loud above our heads. Boring to watch and even more dull to listen to.

I sip water and whiskey.

Chapter 14

Dear Ms. Josephine,

I'm afraid that people have stopped looking at each other. These times are like an R&B song called "strained spines and loneliness." We get all dressed up, but no one notices anyone until we post ourselves on a screen. People have stopped talking and stopped touching anything but their phones. It's dull and hard to watch. That's why I build bookshops. I'm heading to your city, where I hope people are still people to a certain extent. Do lovers still lock eyes or is that a thing of the past? Do friends still laugh at each other's jokes, hug, pat backs? Do families still gather? Do coworkers still go out for beer? Looking forward to hanging out in Paris with you.

Here's to the people-watching capital of the world.

So much to write about there.

Thanks for all you do for me.

Love,
Jeannine

Chapter 15

"I'll take the check," I tell the muscular waiter when my ten minutes to write are over. I snap him out of his screen trance, and he looks thankful for human connection. I ask him if there's a back way upstairs for the awards ceremony so I can avoid the crowd.

"I got you," he says. "Your drink's on me." He refills my cup like I saved him from something in his phone, or maybe he senses I need another drink. "Have this and I'll take you up."

I sip fast, fan slow. I am hoping the preliminary niceties are over and the ceremony has begun.

"Shall we?" he says, extending his bulky arm to me.

"We shall."

I step inside the ballroom as my category, Entrepreneur of the Year, is being announced. The place is packed, airless, chaotic—we are sardines in a boozy tin can. The sound system is glitching. And of course, the AC here is also broken. People are drinking cocktails for relief. Hair sticks to foreheads. Hot breath and anticipation fill the standing-room-only space.

Four women are nominated for the Entrepreneur of the Year award. We all work hard and know each other. They recap our work in pictures, but only one person can win this race.

I find a corner near an outlet so I can charge my phone and fan myself. But before I plug in, my name is called, and the room explodes in applause and cheering. I drop my phone.

"Jeannine, are you here somewhere?" the MC calls out from the stage. "I thought I saw her come in." I'm down on the ground. I could stay down here forever hidden in the crowd, but someone grabs me by the arm. I think she is a reporter. A short-haired woman who loves science fiction. I have seen her in the bookshop many times—I know her genre, just not her name.

"You've won," she tells me as I pick up my phone. She has the perfect smile—warm and peachy. "They are calling you." She stands me up.

The crowd continues clapping only louder as I appear out of nowhere. The reporter waves and points at me so everyone knows I'm still there. All eyes on me. I feel the internal fight begin. It's the heart rate that rams up my throat. She escorts me to the front of the room. Her clammy arm sticks to mine.

"Remember that first day," she whispers, and I recall the first day we met.

The morning I opened Harriett's in 2020, I was greeted by a news truck. This same warm reporter with the perfect peachy smile was sent to cover the opening for Black History Month. Then we got a call from the Fishtown Business District; they wanted to do a ribbon-cutting with members of Congress. The *Philadelphia Inquirer* was sending a documentarian to capture the day's events. Then the neighborhood café wanted to bring coffee, and a group of local farmers wanted to bring fruit, and a florist wanted to bring flowers, and it went on and on like that the day of the opening, with folks offering offerings, and me saying yes on behalf of Ms. Harriett.

It would have been too much for me, but it was not too much for her. She deserves all her praises and more. I had a feeling Harriett's Bookshop was going to make it someway and somehow. I just felt like things would work out. That if I did my part, Ms. Harriett would meet me halfway. I had a feeling people would show up. I just had no idea to what degree.

"You've come a long way," the reporter says as she walks me to the stage. "I love the pink suit too. It's so you. It's so brave."

We navigate through the sea of people. And just as we approach the stage—BOOM!

I grab my ears and duck, not sure of what's happening. Everyone is looking around. The mic has blown. Static. Harriett has a sense of humor. She saves me again. I get handed my award very quickly as the technicians work on the sound. No acidic chalk in my mouth. No electric butterflies in my belly. No speech. No story. I go to the bathroom after all the high fives and hugs to wash my hands. Then slip back out through the bar lobby. Wave goodbye to my bulky waiter friend and leave.

I won.

Well, books won. Ms. Harriett won.

I write a note to myself asking why I have to get so anxious about this sort of event, but I am glad I pushed through and still went.

John texts me he'll be almost done with construction the next day with a winking emoji.

I smile and sleep deeply thinking about all the progress we're making.

Chapter 16

The next morning, I walk-run from my apartment in Society Hill to Fishtown, ignoring the threat of torrential rain. Society Hill where I live is one of the oldest residential neighborhoods in Philadelphia. It was once the home to Lenape people and was likely covered in 100-foot white oak trees before it was settled upon by Quakers in the early 1600s. The architecture is Georgian and Greek Revival, and we still have some original cobblestone streets.

Philly is quieter today. She's sultry and gray. She slows me down and invites me to take in the music of her streets.

I walk so slow that it takes me twice as long to get to the bookshop, and when I am almost there a torrential storm rains down, so now I am soaking wet.

When I arrive at Harriett's, no one is there to greet me. No contractors. No hammers. No paint. No John. He has not finished the floors, the walls, or anything.

I call John, no answer.

Construction is three days behind schedule, and this is the third time in three weeks he's gone missing, only to return with a mouthful of sweet nothings. Everything is halfway done, yet John and his crew are nowhere to be found.

I call John again. No answer.

The walls have no drywall. The bathroom has no door. I have no customers and no place to go pee. The bookshop is suffering. I feel homeless (again!).

I call John. No answer.

Then I turn around and notice he has cocked my favorite three-foot-tall hand-drawn Harriett Tubman portrait on its side and broken the frame. A small match can ignite a blaze.

Call again, no answer.

I start to see red. Everything is undone. I'm not mad, I'm ballistic. I start slow. I hurl half a box of contractor bags this way, rip half a wall of wallpaper that way. This is what it looks like when I am enraged.

I'm so tired of the Johns of this world. And the more I think about it, the more I become inflamed. I want to gather myself but instead I get frustrated that I'm frustrated and fling more things. All of a sudden, it's demolition day. I knock over half a soda can that's filled with half-smoked cigarette butts. NO SMOKING. I scream. NO SMOKING. NO SMOKING. NO SMOKING.

I told John no smoking. But Johns don't listen, they just pretend to listen. They are perpetual line crossers because they don't hear anything that's said. They mistake kindness for weakness. Heat flares from my veins.

I'm tired of the Johns and their disrespect. I smash an incense holder to the ground and ashes fly up in my face. The taste of burnt nag champa lingers on my lips.

I bang piano keys just to hear a noise louder than the one in my head. It sings, "The roof. The roof. The roof is on fire, we don't need no water, let this motherf****r burn!"

Ms. Harriett looks at me sideways, but I think she understands.

She once prayed a man would die for trying to take her freedom. He didn't wake up the next morning. It taught her a lesson in the swift power of her tongue. She doesn't say a thing.

I walk past the front window to pick her painting up off the floor and don't see myself. I see my father's father as my reflection. It's like he's calling my name.

"Jeannine."

It's scary being haunted by that which runs through your veins.

"What are you doing here?" I ask. Then shake my head no at him. I am not gonna start speaking to things I am not supposed to see or hear. He shakes his head no. Some ghosts come to remind you of what you already know. I step closer and closer to see if my eyes are playing tricks on me. He doesn't move. My grandfather was a strict man. In this apparition he is twelve foot tall and dressed in all black like the grim reaper, only with hair slicked back with Dax and a wide jaw. The rage of my shadow self dissipates as his presence looms.

I remember one of the only stories my father told me about his father was how he was raised by sharecroppers on a farm in Sumter, South Carolina. We still aren't sure of his real name because he had to change it when he killed a plantation owner for calling him out of his name. I imagine him cursing and seething, then choking that man to death. My grandfather spent the rest of his life on the run because of a quick decision and a fit of rage. We are the product of him. He looks like my father, just taller and broader. The three of us look more alike than I realize. Taunted by similar demons, like triple flames.

Beautiful words take us places and disrespectful words get us kicked out of places. I remember catching a cheating ex-boyfriend in a lie and breaking a mug on the side of his head.

Not because he cheated but because of something disrespectful he said. "You're just so broken," he said before I bopped him. What if I'd killed him and lodged ceramic glass in his brain?

The thought is chilling.

No way. I shake my head nope. Nope. Nope. Can't go down that road.

My phone rings and pulls me back to reality. I see the name on the screen and my blood returns to a boil.

"John." I steady my voice. I ask the goddess Isis to steady my hands.

"Hi, sweetcakes," John says.

Breathe in Lorene's gentle, tentative surge of gratitude.

"Yes, my love. You called me?" John acts like everything is okay.

"John." I try to find the right words. They seethe out. "I am not your sweetcakes."

This is typical of the Johns of this world. They try to make you feel insane and act like it's okay.

"I was just about to call you," he says.

"John, no one is working. Harriett's is a mess. We only have a few days . . ."

"I know. I know. Sweetca . . ." He catches himself. "The guys will be back next week."

"Next week?" I repeat in shock and pandemonium.

"Anyone can build a bookshop, my love."

This is also typical of the Johns. They lie to everyone including themselves, then when they get caught they shift the blame. Shift the blame. Shift the blame.

"John, I am not your love. I am not your sweetcakes. I am your client. I am looking at the bookshop and there is no way."

"Perhaps this is a spiritual test for you. You must believe. Just keep the faith." I imagine him with a crooked smirk. Nothing worse than people who use spirituality to manipulate. "If you make another payment, my crew will have incentive to work harder and faster for you. Another thousand?"

My grandfather's looming presence reminds me to slow down. Shut up. React. But don't overreact. The Johns will try to make you crazy, this dog will try to take you off track . . . My grandfather says stay sane.

"John, according to our contract, you've terminated your end of our agreement."

"Excuse me?"

"And unfortunately, while I really wanted to work with you and your crew, lack of integrity has set our relationship ablaze."

There's nothing demons hate more than a cool head.

"What about payment for my receipts? And my tools."

"That will have to come out of your deposit."

"My deposit? I promise we can finish this job in a few hours," he insists.

"I promise you, you cannot."

"I bet you'll be begging me to come back," he says out the side of his forked lips.

"Let's bet your tools on it. They'll be outside waiting for you when you come next week, that's if Fishtown doesn't get to them first. Thanks again for today's spiritual lesson, John. Class dismissed."

I release the tightness in my jaw, let my shoulders roll back. I hang up and head over to pick up Harriett off the floor. She and I catch eye contact. Her neck is still held high, despite a broken frame. I take the painting into our cool dark basement—the Underground where she will be protected from ruin, debris, and the Johns of this world.

It's only 9:30 in the morning, I think after sitting in the breeze of the Underground where I once built a darkness book exhibit designed to be experienced by candlelight. When visitors arrived, they were handed a votive and the experience was explained. "Imagine the times in history where people have had to hide to read. Times when readers could be maimed or killed for being found with a single book. There's a story of Harriett going back on one of her missions to rescue a cousin, only to find out he'd been arrested because they found a copy of *Uncle Tom's Cabin* in his cabin. This has happened many times throughout history. The banning of books is ever present; our exhibit is called 'A Cautionary Tale.'"

When folks emerge from the Underground we ask them for one word to describe their experience searching for books and reading by candlelight. "Chilling," "haunting," "claustrophobic," "scary," "hard," "destabilizing," "maddening," various customers have said.

Down there in the dark presence of those who have risked their lives for a chance to read, I am reminded of what's really at stake.

A Shopkeeper knows the risks she must take.

I go back upstairs to pack John's things. I take all the trash out into the rain. I burn another incense and cleanse myself and the shop of bad energy. The incense works, and I never see John again.

While I'm alone in the bookshop listening to thunder and torrential rain, I try to figure out what to do next, and my dad texts me that he doesn't know why I am doing a bookshop named for Josephine Baker.

"What is your obsession, Dad?" I ask.

"There are many braver women in history," he texts.

"I didn't know it was a competition," I double jab back, tired of unsolicited advice.

He tells me he's set up an account so he can order books from Harriett's online and send them to me because he's reading about a woman named Elizabeth Jennings Graham. I've never heard of her.

I thank him and tell him to go back and study World War II and the role Josephine played. But I don't think it's what she did that intrigues me, it's her spirit.

"She was an entertainer," he texts back. Elizabeth Jennings Graham, she was damn near a saint.

"Josephine Baker did more than entertain, Dad. She was a free spirit, self-possessed, a spy like yourself. She was brave."

"Spy?" he questions with an emoji question mark. "She was brave in Paris. Not in the United States."

"It was a world war, Dad. What she did was for the world."

"But did she ever help her own little town? Her own people?"

"Her people were worldwide and not just in some small place, Dad."

"You can't forget your own people while you're fighting for the world."

"And you can't forget the world while youre fighting for your people."

My dad doesn't listen, he's biased. I think Baker reminds him of my mother—beautiful, talented, smart, calculated, and unable to be pinned down.

"Elizabeth resisted on her own block in Brooklyn. Anyone can run away but fighting and sticking through for your home, now that's brave."

He quickly adds that he's back in the hospital because his potassium is low. He's cramping all over. But he plans on getting out of the hospital in a few. It's like he's awaiting freedom papers from his master again. "Any day now. Any day now," I joke.

"Food is god awful here," he complains. "Like leftover slop from yesterday."

"A banana a day keeps the doctors away," I send with a banana emoji.

"Not in my case. Remember Elizabeth Jennings," he makes me promise.

"I will, Dad." I say her name. "Elizabeth Jennings Graham. Elizabeth Jennings Graham."

He calls me. Perhaps he senses something. "How are things?" he asks. He always asks the same questions.

"They're okay."

"Just okay?" He catches on quickly.

"Okay, well the truth is . . ."

My dad loses interest, and he cuts me off mid-sentence. Or maybe it's a tactic he uses to help shift my mindset to something more optimistic.

Lazarus reminds me of the hundreds of people who gathered in front of Harriett's when we opened. "It was the cold of winter, and you had people gathering for a community—what did you call it?"

"It was called a blessingway."

"How'd you get all those people out there doing that?" he asks.

"I don't know." I've told him so repeatedly over the last few years the same thing. I didn't do anything. People just came. The answer doesn't change. But he likes to reminisce.

"There were a lot of people there though," he reminds me again.

"I know, Dad."

"And most of the people there, you'd never met before, right?"

"Right, never."

"So, they came because they were inspired. They saw that article that said, 'she was told not to open a bookshop in Fishtown, but she did it anyway.'"

"They were inspired by the spirit," I correct him.

"It was such an eclectic crowd of families, elders, teenagers." And then he asks me again about the opening circle we did outside with the community before we opened. It's his favorite part of the story.

"It was a blessingway," I tell him again.

"Right right. A blessingway."

Traditionally, a blessingway is an indigenous ceremony performed on new mothers before they birth their firstborn. It acts as a rite of passage marking the singular experience where one moves from maiden to mother. But I had never seen anyone do a blessingway on a bookshop before, so we made it up because it did feel like I was giving birth. We asked folks to gather outside. A storyteller handed each person in the circle a small rock and requested they endow it with a blessing for the space. People passed rocks around to anyone who wanted one. Then we invited each person to call out the name of an ancestor they'd like to see uplifted in our space.

Someone in the crowd called on the name Harriett Tubman, but I already knew she was there with me. She always is. I called on another woman, Ida B. Wells, not knowing that a year later, we would be doing this again, building another bookshop in her name with a new group of neighbors gathered in a similar way.

Others continued around the circle calling out family members, loved ones, and historic figures. And then I heard a familiar voice and to my complete and total shock—this is the part of the story he really likes to hear.

"What happened next?" he texted.

I turned around and in the crowd was my dad (when he could still walk on two legs). He was calling on my own great-grandmothers, Maggie May Cook and Thomasina Reese, whose photos I had hanging on the walls of the bookshop. And he was calling on his own father, James. It was like he was calling on himself because they have the same name.

"Daddy?" I mouthed to him through the crowd. "What are you doing here?"

"I love this," he mouthed back, and then he gave me his big crooked cheesy smile. I called him up to the front to help me cut the ribbon.

The group closed out the blessingway with a call and response, where we declared Harriett's to be a place for peace, love, and respect for everyone. And that is what it's been. I told anything that was not of that spirit not to enter or stay.

Then I hugged my dad's thin, frail frame and whispered a thank you to him for always reading books about spies when I was younger and coming all that way. He laughed a proud hehehe. "Anytime, baby, anytime."

My father had traveled all night by Greyhound bus from Virginia to Philadelphia to surprise me at the opening. He wore a fedora hat and floor-length coat over a navy-blue suit and white tee shirt. He had the quintessential bop of someone who was raised in Brooklyn in the seventies.

He stood beside me as I cut the ribbon and officially opened the doors to the shop. We let hundreds and hundreds of people (and their ancestors) in while one of my favorite DJs played reggae, house, and Afropop music.

"I can't believe your mother didn't come," he said, which made me think for a minute that's why he was really there.

Nearly all the books were sold that day, except for the Lorene Cary *Ladysitting* books that I refused to sell so we'd have some for her reading at Harriett's the next day.

"It was beautiful what you did," he reminded me.

I told him I hadn't done anything; it was all the spirit of Ms. Harriett.

And the writing?

"It's okay."

"Yeah, it'll be okay."

I don't tell him how his father appeared to me. That's a story for another time and place.

"Alright, Number 2. Have a good one."

I look at his profile picture on my phone. Clean cut, tight skinned, and timeless. He always looks the same. If he's making jokes, I know he'll be okay. Alright, Lazarus, speak soon.

I get another text that makes my day: the officials in South Jersey are giving us the Scottish Rite Theater with 1,000 seats to host Nikole Hannah-Jones.

Breathe out. Everything will be okay.

Chapter 17

That night I'm at home alone reading the part of *Ladysitting* where Lorene hops on a plane to confront the insurance company that's holding up care for her nana's much-needed condition. I am in my near-empty apartment dozing off when someone knocks hard.

I open the door. Try to greet her sweetly. I know her well, though I have not seen her in some time.

"You have something for me." Mrs. Graves doesn't say hello. I try to hand her my copy of *Ladysitting*, but that doesn't work. She gets straight to the point. I picture Graves' disease as a tall woman with big hips and big breasts, big hair and big thighs, and a bit of an odor—like a scary stinky blues singing ex-lover. She's come to visit because I stayed out late and though I got her prescription, I didn't fill it. I try to explain about my negligence, my crazy time with John and the rain. But she doesn't want to hear it. Hell hath no fury like a woman scorned. She barges in. She opens my empty fridge. Looks around like a judgmental bitch. She knows I haven't been eating much or going to the gym. I've just been reading and working, working and reading and trying to write something.

"When I'm at home, I want to sit still. When I'm at work, I want to keep moving. There is no in-between."

She rolls her eyes and shakes her head disapprovingly as she circles around me.

"You want some tea?" I ask, trying to calm her nerves and my own. I try to get her to take a seat. I boil her some lavender tea and pour it in her favorite yellow "Let It Be" mug.

"Honey?" I ask.

But just when she's starting to chill, slip off her shoes, and put her big, calloused feet up to relax, I get ahead of myself and ask her if we can hang out some other time, maybe. I just want to shower and go to bed, I wasn't expecting a date night. Really, I want to read. Perhaps I should have said I want to write. "I'll get you your meds in the morning," I promise.

She seems okay. It's like she's in a good place and calmer from the lavender tea. More understanding. Less demanding. She smiles and stands up, dusts herself off like she's good and ready to leave. Leans in, gives me a two-cheek kiss and a massive hug, but Mrs. Graves doesn't let go. She holds me tight for too long in my living room. When I least expect it, she lets go but yanks me back by the nape of my neck and drags me toward the bedroom by the back of my hair.

"You just so damn hardheaded," she reminds me. *I should not have said that*, I think to myself again.

She pulls and pushes me around the small bedroom and then over to my perfectly made bed that I never touch, so I never have to remake it, but she doesn't care about my house rules. She throws me down and stuffs my face into my pillows, destroying months of premade perfection. She lets me back up for air, but not for long.

"I don't want to kill you," she says. "Just make sure you get the lesson." She smacks me around the room again and then pushes me back onto the rumpled bed. All the while reminding me that I deserve this because I don't listen. She mounts me and holds me there, punishing me for hours under her weighted funky grip. I can't walk or talk when she acts this way. I'm suffocating and my legs are flailing, and I can't breathe. My heart is rushing and unsettled. I can't. I can't. I can't. Mrs. Graves wants an all-nighter with me. She wraps her thighs around my neck and holds me tight between her knees like a wrestler. My eyes can move but they cannot see. I am barely conscious. I can think but I cannot hold a thought. I cannot hear.

I remember fourteen years ago when I first met Mrs. Graves. I had gone to Trinidad and Tobago to visit my mother's younger sister, my auntie Ann Marie. Another Marie. Auntie Ann Marie told me about a relationship she had with an inherited siren that she nicknamed Mrs. Graves—which was short for thyrotoxicosis. You could see it in my aunt's eyes; just saying the name was tiring.

Auntie Ann Marie is the slenderest of my aunts, with a teeny tiny waist and large behind. She has long brown hair and the family's trademarked oversized forehead. Her skin is taut and rich. She's lived in the same six-story walk-up for the last fifty years. She is smart and tries to tell me many things, but she speaks in parables and stories and patois and make-believe—like a prophet.

"Mrs. Graves does make ya go tin tin tin cause she wan' eat all ya food. And she does make ya wan' move fas' fas' fas' like so, to do all she work and she wan' make ya see tings no one else does wan' see. She does visit one woman in we family every generation, ya know. Now she wan' visit you it seems."

Auntie Ann Marie knows Mrs. Graves well. My aunt cooks for me all day, makes me saltfish and bake for breakfast, makes me curry and chicken and rice and oxtails and callaloo and salad for lunch. She walks up and down her six flights of steps between cooking for me, helping a dozen other people from all over Port of Spain. She feeds them and clothes them and hands out books and sanitary wipes and cleaning supplies. Auntie Ann Marie holds a community meeting, writes a letter of recommendation, sews three uniforms, makes a balloon arrangement; she is raising lots of children, so kids are in and out. She is checking homework and doing art projects and folding laundry before she has to go to church where she is an usher. She never makes a single complaint. She is domestic in ways that my mother is not. They look alike, but she is motherly in ways that my mother is not.

"Complainin' is de work of de devil. It's Satan usin' ya own tongue against ya," my auntie Ann Marie says.

I tell her I want to go to church with her that evening and see how the Shango Baptist praise. "We does praise Gawd de way everyone else does," she tells me. But I don't think so. The Shango Baptist are a group specific to the Caribbean who blend West African spiritual practices, Yoruba culture, and Pentecostal traditions. It's something I'd love to write about someday, I tell her. "Write about ya self, Jeannine, don' write bout we," she laughs. Auntie Ann Marie tells me to meet her at church later because she must leave early to set up.

"How do you do it all?" I ask.

"My help cometh from de All mighty spirit."

She tells me I am to wear an all-white dress to church and a white bra and panties. The only white clothes I have are oversized linen pants, which I thought no one would notice as long as I sat in the back, but everyone notices all at once as soon as I walk in the church. Auntie Ann Marie sees me and is appalled. She marches me out the front door of the small building onto the street. She quickly changes me into someone else's long white dress right outside as other church mothers stand watch. She wraps my hair in a long white cloth like I am her baby doll.

"I tell ya what to wear, but ya see you? Ya hardheaded and too fas'. At least ya panties is white."

When I am re-dressed, I am permitted into the service as though I was not just stripped naked outside. They behave as if nothing has happened even though it's only a few of us and everyone must know. I can barely understand the preacher as he pants and chants and sings in a thick Trinidadian accent. But as I am about to take my seat, he instructs me, "Do not sit, well-wisher, take up your bed and walk." I understand that, clearly. I am told to come up front and walk counterclockwise in a circle around a huge wooden pole that runs from the ceiling to the floor like a column down the center of the church. As I walk around three times, others join in dancing to the drumming and singing in praise as we walk and walk. He tells more and more people to join me. After a couple more circles around the pole, I get comfortable and kick off my shoes. When everyone in the church including the preacher is going around the circle, we all grow louder and louder, clapping hands and tambourines and maracas, stomping bare feet on the hardwood and yelling as our steps grow faster and faster yet more in sync, and the more we go around the circle, the more I can see what is and what ain't. The thunder is what they call it. And the more I can feel what was and what was not. The fire is what they call it. That is when I first met Mrs. Graves. I noticed her because I was out of breath. She was there between me and my aunt, big hipped and swaying. "She is not someone to fear but someone to respect," my aunt says. Mrs. Graves goes around the circle with us many times into the night and early into the next morning as the service goes on and on. My aunt says Mrs. Graves is part of the family, an inheritance passed down for many generations.

"Get used to she, give she wha she does need and she give you de same damn ting, but if ya see ya starve she, she will starve you worse." My aunt points her finger at my face. "Don' ever make she come lookin' for ya, cause she don' like dat at all at all at all at all."

I wake up. I breathe in the drums still beating from my time in Trinidad.

I fall back asleep thinking about thunder and fire, and it shut up in my bones.

I am back there on the island going around the circle barefoot with the children and the elders and the mothers and the babies being reminded of my lesson—don' let she come lookin' for ya at all at all at all.

I wake up again, but I can't speak. There is no Trinidad. No drums. There is no Auntie Ann Marie. It's just me and Mrs. Graves. She's like the folklore my aunts told us about when we were small, she's my haint.

I fall back asleep and I'm at a beach on the north coast of Trinidad staring at the Caribbean Sea after Auntie Ann Marie's church service. I am watching the splashing waves as the water creeps closer, trying to cool the fire in me. I think of Shango. I am trying to understand what's just happened. The water creeps closer and I'm in the ocean getting wet in someone else's sanctified white dress.

I wake up the next morning tucked beneath my covers in my bed, but I can't move. Even though I can hear my phone buzzing with texts and calls. I can't answer. I can't move heavy boxes; I can't even move my arms. I can't place orders. I am out of order. I'm stuck in bed after a violent all-nighter, yet it's as though Mrs. Graves were never here. She's left no trace. I spend the day in bed thinking about Trinidad and my auntie Ann Marie and Mrs. Graves and being hardheaded. Many people grow upset with me for not responding or coming to their event or giving them my full attention including the bank, but I can't. I can't. I can't.

I spend the day in bed reading the beginning of *Ladysitting* (again!).

A Shopkeeper knows when enough is enough.

Chapter 18

The next morning, I have a call with Joshua from the bank about the purchase of the building. I am buzzing to hear what he has to say about our closing.

"Hey, Jeannine. How are you?"

"I'm good, Josh, ready to close tomorrow, correct?"

He is a great guy, with the most beautiful speech pattern, he wears high-end suits and has great style. "Well, there's some stuff on my end, that . . . frankly we still have more to do, and we are not ready."

"But Josh, I'm leaving for France on Friday, for the next four weeks."

"I know," he sings to lighten the blow.

"Can I sign from Paris, Josh?"

He thinks so but doesn't know. He thinks if I can sign at the embassy, we should be fine.

"Let's just play it by ear," he tells me.

I don't like that. But I thank him. I want to throw the phone, but I thank him again. I remember the phrase "anger covers sadness, sadness covers rage." And it's true I'm sad, not angry. We aren't going to finish the renovation in time. We aren't going to close on the building. And we aren't going to sell any books this summer. My brain is rebelling against itself like a metaphor for my body. I will have to be in two places at once, I decide. I'll clone myself, I joke. Philly in Paris. One me in France and one me in Fishtown; one me has to complete the renovation and operate two bookshops, and the other me must write a novel, which is due in just a few months.

Chapter 19

Dear Ms. Josephine—

I've met another Marie, and I'll see her this summer in Paris. It all started with COVID. She introduced herself as an actor who was donating money to help independent bookstores through the pandemic. She wrote to me via my Instagram DMs. But everyone and their mama was in my DMs at that time—everyone wanted books. I told her I wanted to go give out books at protests. Like what's all this I can't breathe nonsense? We can breathe! I wanted to visit Minneapolis and Kentucky and of course Philly and give out the only thing I had an abundance of—books. I told her whatever she gave me, I'd use it to educate organizers. She loved that. Sent enough for me to buy 100 copies of Harriett Tubman's *Bound for the Promised Land*. I did my thing. But we never met.

Months later she came to the shop, but it was snowing, and I was somewhere else building another bookshop (Ida's) that same day. She'd come through the snow with her elderly mother to meet me and I got caught up in creating and forgot.

All I could do was apologize. It happens. I suspect she was upset, but gracious.

"Maybe next time."

Then she wrote to me one day and told me she'd just moved to Paris from LA to give herself space to flaneuse (the French word for wander about), but check this, she's from Philly and I never knew. And deep down she's a bookish writer. So, we became pen pals, writing letters to each other about our lives and the similarities of our fathers.

She has an apartment of many things in Paris—many colors and many flowers and many trinkets in a home that soars above the Seine. She lets me write there.

Marie tells me she will be in Paris for the Olympics this summer. We will be pen pals, and then see each other when she comes into town.

I wonder where this new Marie will guide me.

> Bonsoir cherie,
> -j

Chapter 20

Before I leave for Paris, I have one more event—"Happy Birthday, Ida," on behalf of Ida's Bookshop in South Jersey.

I sit in the dressing room of the Scottish Rite Auditorium just behind the stage. Everyone is in their places. The youth conductors are downstairs stamping hundreds of books, volunteers have done everything from setting up tote bags to directing traffic to sound design and lighting. There are stilt walkers outside greeting people with a wave. A hula-hooper lady belly dances and gyrates through the line, keeping folks entertained by the sound of a vibraphonist playing "Happy Birthday" on an instrument that vibrates through your bones.

It's a 90-plus-degree day. In less than thirty minutes we have eight hundred people packed into the auditorium waiting to hear Nikole Hannah-Jones speak about the history of New Jersey and Ida B. Wells and the future of books and the role they play in modern day.

Right before I opened Ida's Bookshop in Collingswood, New Jersey, I took a month-long vow of silence to think. At that time it felt like every industry was trying to placate and make money by throwing money at collective pain and I did not want to participate. My mother would go with me every day to sit in the Ida's Bookshop space in silence.

From sunrise to sunset I did not speak or listen to music; all I did was shut up and sit there.

I thought Collingswood would be safe. It was 2021 and most houses in the quaint suburban neighborhood had signs and flags that said Black Lives Matter and No Place for Hate.

For the opening, my older sister, Number 1, came to visit and we created a three-day weekend called Alice in Walkerland, in honor of an interview I had with Alice Walker. I asked a team of local set designers to turn the bookshop into a juke joint.

On Thursday to kick off the weekend, I interviewed Alice Walker about her memoir of journal entries, *Gathering Blossoms Under Fire*. I ask her about gardening and relationships and her longings and criticisms.

I ask her how to be a better sister to my sisters, and she says it's all about listening. "Even when they say things that you don't want to hear."

The radio station gifts copies of books to their members.

On Saturday, I ask Salamishah Tillet to come in and lead a trauma-healing conversation with writing prompts over mimosas and tea because she had just written *In Search of The Color Purple* and also runs an organization alongside her own sister called A Long Walk Home. That night, I asked friends to perform, and others dressed up, and we turned the bookshop into the juke joint from *The Color Purple* all weekend.

And on the Sunday my sister was like a visiting bishop, she even wore a robe to deliver a sermon like the revival in the story's monumental church scene. Instead of a traditional ribbon-cutting ceremony, we held a service in front of the shop that sprawled into the street. I sang "This Little Light of Mine" with a tambourine. Everyone got a copy of *The Color*

Purple twenty-fifth anniversary edition and *Gathering Blossoms Under Fire*.

But once you open a small bookshop in a small town, you get to know your neighbors real quick.

Things got unsafe.

It wasn't long before I began having a back-and-forth with the same mayor who invited me into town in the first place. We could not agree on the installation of a phone booth I had built in Ida's name. It sat outside of the bookshop and didn't obscure anything. I wanted people to go inside and call Ida up and tell her what they wanted. Listen to what she had to say. People loved it. It started a lot of conversation, but the mayor and commissioners hated it and wanted it gone—effective immediately.

"It's bringing people together," I say.

"It's against rule 356487," is all I hear.

I call the NAACP.

"Is there anything I can do about this?"

"Move it."

That was not what I wanted to hear.

I recognize that it is not easy to build a monument to your ancestors in a public space because someone else (perhaps someone counter to your ancestor) has to approve everything and it has to be done their way. I learned that our mayor had been in office for twenty-five years and the town was run like his kingdom. I looked around and realized, like Alice, I was not in Philadelphia anymore. All my decisions needed approval from the king.

I decided one night that I was gonna spend all day and all night monitoring that phone booth because it was in front of my shop and it was time to put my foot down. And I sat in it all day and night. I sat in my car next to it watching that thing like a mother hen. That night I read *The 1619 Project*. And every essay helped me bit by bit. Every essay made me understand the legacy of the warrior spirit. That book helped me get through the night. One day I came back to the bookshop and the phone booth was gone.

But now, five years later, the high school students have staged their second walkout because they say though the community looks pretty on the outside, there's something really ugly inside that needs to be addressed. Cars have been vandalized with messages I don't even want to write. Storefronts are being broken into and hate messages being taped to poles. It was like boils started popping all over the neighborhood's face. The community was in an uproar, so I did the only thing I know how to do: contacted artists, activists, and authors and asked who might be willing to sit in the gap with us. It's one thing to be a celebrity author, artist, or activist, it's another to let your feet do the talking and create a world of real-time measurable social change. Nikole Hannah-Jones said okay right away—not speak to her publisher, or publicist, she was her real self and I was my real self, and she not only understood the need but showed up in word and in deed.

"If we don't do something quickly this neighborhood is likely to implode."

"I got you," she said.

It is not often that an author of her stature comes to small towns. I try to tell publicists and publishers this is a major mistake. You should send authors to small places in obscure places.

I sit in the Scottish Rite Auditorium, I look at myself and thank Ms. Ida B. Wells, because we both know I wouldn't be sitting here if not for her. She always had the guts to ask hard questions and gather answers and organize toward measurable results.

The other gift she's given me in South Jersey is the Haddon Township Equity Initiative, a small group that started off as concerned moms the next town over. I call them the most gangster moms I ever met. From the first year we opened Ida's we have collaborated with them in some way, from dinner, book, and movie nights to wine tastings with their board member who is an ex-sommelier. Now they are here helping to host "Happy Birthday, Ida" with me. They are helmed by my new good friend, Isis Williams.

"Who is helping you?" she calls me up and asks.

"I have about six youth conductors."

"For eight hundred people?"

As a former wedding planner, Isis is the queen of details, and she knows what it takes to host eight hundred people and I do not. She is omniscient, like the goddess whose name she shares and spirit she embodies. I believe I will be sent the right people and I always am.

Isis stepped in and organized everything to a tee; it is the first time in my life that before an event, I am in silence and not nervous and I am finally able to take it all in. I sit in the dressing room of the Scottish Rite Auditorium just behind the stage. Everyone is in their places—and it's time for the fourth birthday of Ida's Bookshop and one hundred sixty-second birthday of Ida B. Wells.

There are not supposed to be tears at birthday parties, but on the last question everyone just starts. One of the youth conductors asks Nikole: "What are we supposed to do about the state of things? We are only children!"

And Nikole says many things, but most impactfully she says through tears, "Prove their asses wrong."

At the end of that conversation, I decide internally that I

need to find a permanent home for Ida's just like we've done for Harriett's. The landlord is increasing the rent annually and we are being priced out of our location. I am going to close the bookshop and build it somewhere else.

> *A Shopkeeper knows she has to own her own building if she wants to sustain. Rent is the silent bookshop killer especially when it increases during a recession.*

Chapter 21

A few days later I am finally sitting on an airplane preparing for takeoff. The person sitting next to me is listening to Lisa Stansfield's "All Around the World" too loud in her headphones. It's 11 p.m. on a red-eye flight and where I typically would've tapped her shoulder and politely asked her to turn it down, this time I let it play.

This song reminds me of my mother and my sisters. We used to spend all of our time together, but then everyone grew up. When I was a little girl, my mother was unable to get a driver's license because doctors declared her legally blind, and yet, she still drove us to get ice cream in her small red hatchback when she decided it was a "good eye day."

She'd blast "Been around the world and I, I, I, I can't find my baby, I don't know, and I don't know why, why he's gone away, and I don't know where he can be, my baby, but I'm gonna find him," when it came on the radio because once again our father was away. We sang along—her three daughters as her chorus—Number 1, Number 2, and Number 3.

"What color is it?" my mother would ask us about the traffic lights as she approached one. We'd all call out "green" or "red" while still singing her favorite song—"Been around the world and I, I, I . . ."

When we got home, our mother, who couldn't read to me,

would have my older sister, Number 1, read to me instead. The only issue was my older sister liked the original Brothers Grimm fairy tales. She read me stories where fairies' wings were singed, and children were boiled alive. My sister would tell me to cover my ears when I was scared, while she continued to read aloud. I'd be balled up infant style, head to my knees as she acted out scenes.

"What's that mean?" I'd ask every few paragraphs. Submerged in the story but stunted by syntax.

"It means he ate the children, Jeannine. It means her tongue was chopped off, Jeannine. It means she was drugged."

We'd dress up in our mother's church clothes, living in fairy worlds where we had to creep through forests to escape wolves and boiling hot cauldrons and villages overrun with rats.

"Cover your eyes," my older sister would say as she looked ahead a few pages at the sketches of a heinous three-eyed little girl. "Come here." I came closer to her. "Do you want to be like Little One Eye or Little Three Eyes?" she asked.

I didn't know any better; I just wanted to survive in the story, so I nodded my head.

"Which one?" she asked again.

"Little One Eye," I said.

"You sure, right?"

I nodded again.

"Sit still," my sister said, laying my head back onto her lap as she applied her "magic oils" to my eye. It was a cold liquid gel across the bottom of my left eye from a needle-thin tube. "Stay still," she repeated.

So I lay there, eyes shut tight with magic oil and body stiff as she read the story of the Grimms' three sisters and their bleating goat.

At the end of the story, when Little Two Eyes goes to marry the Prince, I wanted to see her gown. I went to open my eye and it would not open.

"I told you to stay still," my sister said, shutting the book. I went to grab my eye to yank it open and my fingers got stuck.

"It's stuck!" I let out a terror-filled shriek. "It's stuck!"

"I know," she said matter-of-factly. "You're Little One Eye."

"What did you do?" My mother ran in shouting over my wailing.

"She wanted to be Little One Eye," my sister replied.

"She wanted to be what?" my mother screamed, flinging me over her shoulder and running out the front door.

"Little One Eye," my sister said earnestly once more.

I close my eyes as the song "All Around the World" continues to play in my left ear.

I also remember dancing to that song on my own in the car when I got a bit older. My thirteen-year-old self driving my mother's hatchback to do groceries and run errands because good eye days stopped happening.

Yet my mom was still enrolled in school to get her master's in theology. She would let us drive her to school and talk to me about her classes and let us type her papers and read to her—Number 1, Number 2, and Number 3—even the little one had a turn. I liked the essays about Taoism and ancient Egypt most of all. She got her degree as a blind woman with three children. Even as a blind woman she still traveled all around the world. I even brought her with me to Paris on one of my trips and took her to The American Library of Paris and the twinkling Eiffel Tower. She was fine, but having her with me in Paris nearly gave me a heart attack. I was on the edge when cars and motorcycles and bikes whizzed by. The streets of Paris aren't exactly accessible.

The flight attendant reminds me to put on my seat belt which snaps me back. I do as I am told with a customer service smile.

I am so tired on the flight that it feels like my eyes are glued shut.

I don't recall falling asleep, but I do recall waking up to the sound of a new voice:

"Mesdames et messieurs, bonjour. Le vol 333 à Paris. Nous espérons que vous avez passé un agréable voyage. La température extérieure est de 23 degrés. Réveillez-vous et profitez de la lumière. Nous vous souhaitons un excellent séjour."

Chapter 22

Dear Ms. Josephine—

I'm back! This summer I am not killing myself building an installation at 5 rue de Médicis just to end up in Hospital Saint-Louis with fevers or following Baldwin's footsteps through Provence just to end up in a seedy motel, or hosting a three-day symposium with your daughter, though she is quite sweet—this time I am here to fill my own cup. I am here to transform myself like you did. From Freda McDonald to Josephine Baker. I will stop being The Shopkeeper so I can become Jeannine the Author. Send me signs that you're close by.

-j

Chapter 23

Paris called me; I did not call her. In 2020, Marie sent me a scholarship application for a fellowship to a program that she thought would allow me to trace James Baldwin's footsteps in France. I applied as I was told. I received the scholarship, but the trip was pushed back three years because of COVID. So, I waited in anticipation all those years and didn't get to go until 2023. Though the scholarship program ended up being sketchy, I started to call James Baldwin my uncle Jimmy, because I was following his footsteps around France and Switzerland, and he was the only family I had. As I read his books, I imagined him reading directly to me. He felt like a distant relative who had invited me to their home.

A Shopkeeper listens to her elders.

Everyone listens to Uncle Jimmy, not just me. It was he who told Auntie Maya that she needed to write *I Know Why the Caged Bird Sings* when she said she didn't want to write a memoir. It was he who had the gall to critique Richard Wright. It is his books that keep many bookshops in business and busy. It was following him around that brought me to the idea of Josephine's—a roving bookshop that pops up like Banksy—birthed from my imagination and his declaration that "And once you realize you can do something it is difficult to live with yourself if you don't." Since then, I've been figuring out ways to build Josephine's annually in Paris, from art galleries to friends' homes to Airbnbs.

I am back again. The ride from Orly into the 13th arrondissement reminds me of the ride into Society Hill from PHL. The two cities are twin sisters. Like Philly, Paris is colorful and architecturally stunning, historic and musical and funny, but she also has her ways about her. All too often folks favor one sister over the other, or only visit one sister and not the other, when in fact they are as much different as they are the same. You need to meet them both to understand what I mean.

Chapter 24

The great mother, Isis, has sent me a woman who was born and raised in Philadelphia. Her name is Camille, and she has been living in Paris since the mid-eighties. She speaks French, she speaks Paris, she speaks global history and migration and math, but most important for me she speaks Philly—albeit a Mt. Airy, upper-middle-class Philly, but she speaks Philly just the same. She spits the slowest, dopest, most Appalachian-style storytelling with rhythm and reason.

She has one poem that she calls "Motherology" about the study of mothering. When I say the great mother Isis sent me her, and her me, I mean one day I go to dinner with the head of WURD Radio, Sara Lomax-Reese, and the head of everything else, Tayyib Smith. I mention I'm heading to Paris to build Josephine's and Sara across from me says, well then you need to know my sister friend, Camille, and she connects us right then via email. When I got home from dinner, I had another email from Penelope Fletcher, the owner of The Red Wheelbarrow, an anglophone bookstore in Paris. Penelope is writing to say, I need to meet this woman, her friend, Camille. And when I wake up in the morning a third woman who I barely know has sent me an email saying it's best I be in touch with a woman she knows named Camille as soon as possible. Both of us are cc'd.

This is how the great mother moves when you pay attention.

I email this woman Camille, and we hop on the phone. We both agree that the signs don't get more glaring. She even knows my agent, Ms. Marie, who agrees we should meet.

After a few conversations, I realize Camille is the next conductor on my Overground Underground Railroad. She is one of many people who will open up their homes to me. They give me safe passage and a place to rest.

Soon after our first call, Camille and I decide I will spend the summer writing the first draft of my novel in her home, which she has nicknamed La Porte Bleue—meaning the blue door. "The monks come here," she tells me of the Tibetan monks who meditate in her adjacent garden. "And so will you."

All I had to do was find a grant that would help fund the plan. We touch and agree.

Then I apply for one BINC grant specifically for booksellers working on their first novels, which I felt sure was made for me, but I don't get it. I don't get discouraged. Well, I do, but not for long. I ask Ms. Josephine and Uncle Jimmy and Ms. Harriett and my grandmothers and great-grandmothers on both sides to help make a way for me. The way has already been made, they say. A few weeks later, I receive the Cultural Treasures Award.

Philly finally loves me back, I think. I get to spend the summer preparing to interview Lorene Cary about her memoir in the fall, in addition to writing my debut novel. I get to live in Paris for the summer.

"What do you want to do in Paris?" Camille asks.

"I want to write my book," I tell her.

"What do you need to write your book?"

"I need everyone to shut up," I laugh.

She laughs and agrees. But I wonder what that really means

and why I feel the need to fly across the world to Philly's unofficial sister city.

Stay present, Camille reminds me, calming my wandering mind. "What do you want from Paris?"

No one has ever asked me what I wanted from a city.

I had never even thought of it. I like Paris because she is Philly's quieter older sister. They feel alike and they look the same; she makes me feel at home, just differerently.

I didn't tell Camille that back home I left Philly and the bookshop and the building purchase in complete disarray. She's a Virgo and she worries like one. I tell her I need quiet space—a library. A Quaker meeting house. A good place for a drink. A boulangerie. A café. A restaurant with Wi-Fi that stays open late. And water.

"Want to see the Olympics?!"

"Absolutely not."

"Art galleries?"

"Not this trip."

"Fashion?"

"I'm only bringing like two outfits."

"Okay, make a list of libraries you want to visit . . ."

"I'll work at the closest library. I don't need to visit a bunch. I'm not a tourist. Pretend I live here."

"Oh, that's perfect," Camille tells me. "The BNF is across from Josephine Baker's pool."

"What's that?" I ask because it sounds like a sign.

"A floating pool on top of the waters of the Seine." There are also solariums, saunas, a hammam, a jacuzzi, and a fitness room in there.

"My cup runneth over," I proclaim.

"Not yet." She smiles.

Walking distance from her house happens to be the National Library of France. The Bibliothèque nationale de France (BNF) is the largest repository of French writing in the world. It rests on the southern bank of the Seine. The library is composed of four 25-story glass towers that surround a large forest-garden in the center and a gazillion books, many that I can only admire but not read because they are mostly written in French.

"There are other things I'd like to show you while you're here." She speaks low and slow. "Sacred things for your asylum."

"So this trip is not about the Eiffel Tower." We both laugh. "It's not about croissants and flowery language and French love affairs?"

"It's about what it's about."

"Some cliches are deep."

"Right on."

"It is."

"Well okay."

And now I've landed, and I'm headed to La Porte Bleue as planned.

Chapter 25

To get to Camille's house, you can't be afraid to traverse a dark alley with overgrown cypress trees and berry vines that grow just above your head and make you crouch down as you walk. This is a rite of passage, a gate of no return. When you finally stand up at the end of the alley, you enter through a creaky blue gate to a two-story house with another blue door. All around you are bursts of kissing green trees, bamboo, and lilacs that I've just missed in full bloom. Camille is there standing in her garden, tall, a former model with a multicolored silk head wrap and thick silver jewelry. She is soft spoken and slow moving and bilingual but very straightforward. She forces me to listen. *A Jawn in her Jardin*, I think. Philly in Paris. She tells me about the lilac tree and the Nina Simone song, about Nina's time in Philadelphia where her genius was rejected by the Curtis Institute of Music and her time in Paris where she once lived in this same arrondisement. She tells me about the many creatives like me who have entered through her gates and sat there at the table in her jardin as a rest stop on their way back home.

"I provide asylum." She lights one of the cigarettes I've bought her through duty free. The ones her mom used to smoke. "Can't get these here," she tells me as she inhales and exhales—they are a Philly thing. We sit across from one another and stare into nature.

She's been raised a Quaker school lifer, which brings out the Quaker in me. But now she's Quaker French. Stunning in her simplicity. Which I hope she brings out in me too. Quieter. More pensive. I only bring one colorful, long, lightly knit duster. She fawns over it—it's vintage and it matches her home—filled with 1960s and '70s midcentury Philadelphia memorabilia and masks and music figurines and teak wood and velvet pillows and a large Buddha statue. "I plan to wear it over everything," I say about my duster as I swing it like a cape.

We discuss our shared connection to the Quakers. Before the bookshop, I'd been working for the American Friends Service Committee in Philadelphia and then was hired in Washington to write the human rights curriculum for DC Public Schools. The Religious Society of Friends, better known as the Quakers, first came to Philadelphia from England in the 1600s. They brought with them their values of simplicity, peace, integrity, community, equality, and stewardship. Designing that curriculum took me down a rabbit hole into Aristotle and Socrates and Locke and Rousseau and Maat and Ubuntu—what does it mean to be an individual in a community and what are our rights and responsibilities to ourselves and each other? What is man's law and what is universal law and what are the personal laws of ethics and morality? How does a pacifist fight for what they believe in?

My work with the Quakers sent me abroad to Nairobi, Kenya, and Birmingham, England, for free, so although I am not a Quaker, I always considered myself a friend of The Friends. The more I learn about their values, the more I translate them into action in the world. Anyone can experience the divine they believe, and revelations happen all the time. I agree. "Quakers

[are] almost as good as colored. They call themselves friends and you can trust them every time," Ms. Harriett is falsely quoted as having said in the late 1800s as they were often her co-conspirators in getting folks free. And now I have Camille, a stunning co-conspiratorial Philly Quaker all the way in Paris giving me a place to hide out.

Even though I haven't been with The Friends in the five years since I've opened the bookshops, I find myself asking for a meeting house, which we have everywhere in Philadelphia. But none in Paris during the summer, she tells me. But you don't need a meeting to access silence, you don't need a meeting to access the divine. You don't need a meeting for revelation. All of it can happen anywhere, with anyone or all on your own or at the same time. There in Camille's jardin we sit silent for a bit under the lure of Paris's evening light peeking through her sycamore trees.

"I got you a beer," she says, running into the house and then back out. Opening the ice-cold drink she says, "It's called Number Nine." She points to the blue beer packaging. Then she reminds me my name Jeannine is—on purpose—Jean NINE. "The signs don't get no clearer than that. I'm gonna call you Nine. May I?"

"I like that."

That's better than Number Two. I laugh to myself thinking about my dad.

"It's all in the math," Camille says. "And your math is mathing, Number 9." Her father, Dr. L. Waldo Rich, was a Temple University scholar and mathematician, but he died when she was still young. We talk about his work teaching math to troubled youth and how math is a universal language of truth. I tell her I'm bringing fifteen Philly youth to Paris in a few months for the same reason that her father went into communities to teach—because if we don't who will? "How you like that math?"

I look up the number 9. Some people say the ninth life is the last one, like cats in ancient Egyptian mythology and Shakespearean plays. The last life is about the art of learning how to allow everything you need to come your way. You watch it unfold in perfect order—but the trick is you can't force anything to happen, you have to just wait. The rule is of patience. Some say cats have nine lives and old souls and after the ninth life, they have learned all the lessons they've come to acquire and are finally free to head home. The last lesson is the most important one.

We laugh into the night and eat tapas and drink number 9s.

"Welcome to La Porte Bleue."

Chapter 26

I try to sleep, but can't sleep because I am still on Philly time. So I write a note to myself:

Dear Jeannine:

Remember that time a guy came to the bookshop like a normal customer and then randomly you ran into him at a Shakespeare & Company downtown, and it was so weird like he was cheating on your bookshop but also it was like you were cheating on your bookshop too. And you know how you are about the signs, you assumed it was fate.

One night he comes into Harriett's and starts reading one of your poems out loud from your book and it's the worst one you could think of—the one where it starts "I've never been in love, it's always been a lie, I'm a cat toy a play thing, a forget me not." So yeah, the worst one.

And you're thinking this is what Roberta Flack was talking about because he's killing you softly. Why would you ever publish that thing? The future is gonna be like TMI.

In no time you are sneaking him Heavenly Bites,

a cookbook and ingredients—but you never EVER touch, not a hug or a handshake—you never even look each other in the eye. You maybe once patted him on the shoulder while you were laughing. Big mistake.

You were breaking all the rules just being in the bookshop together as he wasn't allowed to be in the same room with a woman alone and you were in the bookshop until 4 a.m. talking sonnets.

You put him on to Gwendolyn Brooks, who in one of her love poems says:

"Your arms are water."

He put you on to al-Mutanabbi who says:

"If you ventured in pursuit of glory, Don't be satisfied with less than the stars."

You eat curried lamb with raisins cross-legged on the floor in the back of the bookshop while y'all dissect line by line. You two speak poems in code.

There's a Somali poem that he taught me called "Has Love Been Blood-Written" by Hadraawi and it's about this guy who wrote a letter to a singer but he used his actual blood as ink. And in the poem he's saying this is true love. It asks would you give your lover a letter written in your blood? Can you sit in silence with your lover? Can you wait 1,000 days to be with them? And some mornings he texts you "Good morning" and you respond 27 or 32, which is the number of days you've known each other as you imagine 1000 days with him.

So you're thinking clearly you are in love, right? Like you don't read someone's poems out loud to them unless you're getting married. You don't bring a woman chai tea at 3 a.m. just because.

On day 64 you wrote him a love letter—not in blood, but still a really long love letter. He never replied. On day 75 he drew you a flower. You thought that was sweet.

On day 89 you wake to a text that says he's married someone. Just like that. No warning. No context. You're like what???? Huh!?? How? We are talking every day and sneaking each other naan? How'd she get in front of me? But his marriage only lasted a few weeks—def not 1,000 days.

He calls you one night like I prob have some crazy disease now. And it don't matter to you because we don't touch anyway and you just go right back to your late-night philosophical rendezvous.

But every few days he feels so guilty and he tells you he can't do this anymore. You say okay. Out of respect and then he's right back at your door with more biryani and more al-Mutanabbi.

"I can't run around with the lady from the bookstore at night," he'd say. You understood. You respected it.

But get this—the part you won't believe—one day you found a book, called *Judgment Day* by Rasha al Ameer. The book is about a religious man who falls in love with a woman researcher outside of the faith because they are translating al-Mutanabbi together and his whole life falls apart when the community finds out what he's done. He chose love over love of religion. Unlike you, that researcher in the book actually gets to be touched. You ordered the book to read together, but that book summary was the final nail.

That Friday he called you and said I'm really done this time and you never heard from him again. It's better than being on again and off again.

You finished that book, *Judgment Day*, on your own and it turns out the religious leader and the researcher have a beautiful lifelong love together in that story.

Chapter 27

The next morning, I wake up to sunshine because Paris is always lit just the right way, and she feels breezy like a river of running water, and jasmine bushes outside of my new window smell like spring. I grab a banana and water and begin my twenty-minute trek to the BNF—my new neighborhood librarie.

"Just walk toward the water, Nine. You can't miss it," Camille tells me like it's my first day of school.

I arrive at Piscine Josephine Baker, the pool of Josephine Baker, which sits at the foot of the library. I am in the right place. I look into the water and see my own face. This year's Josephine's Bookshop is only for one person. It's me.

I walk up what feels like a mountain of stairs in a heat that can only be softened by the Seine. My heavy leather boots have traversed canyons and beaches, forests and swamps, and now they are about to climb me to the top of the largest library in Paris. I pass teams of TikTok dancers, intense security, and French speakers, until I find a table in the back near the café and the bathrooms to write. I love public silence. I find a gray couch and stare at my computer, but nothing happens. Nothing comes out. I made it this far and now nothing. I open my phone to the note section and write the first line of my novel.

"Once upon a time . . ." My thumbs hover over the screen for a moment. A fairy tale, I think to myself, no an allegory, my other self says. "Once upon a time . . . there was a shopkeeper who did like touch."

My dad calls just as I finish my first sentence. I don't answer. I put my phone on do not disturb. I can't be a good daughter right now. I crawl up on a gray couch in the middle of the library. I am sure people are wondering who comes to the library just to sit on their phone, *tres Americain*, but that's how the first five pages spill out like a long text message. I start with my meet cute, the name for the scene when two love interests meet at the beginning of a romance. In my first draft The Shopkeeper was named Jeannine and it was based off of a time I recalled sitting in Harriett's and a customer coming in, picking up my book, *Conversations with Harriett*, and reading a passage from own book out loud—it was mortifying and gratifying. I thought it was the perfect way to start a book about a bookshop that was not quite open yet. And that's how the novel began.

Chapter 28

That evening, my conductor, Camille, insists I visit the local Cameroonian restaurant, Moonlight, for dinner. "It's the closest thing you'll get to soul food around here." She gives me a list of dishes to try: "Poulet means chicken, gambas are shrimp, boeuf is beef, but my favorite appetizer is the mouton y riz, lamb over rice." Reminds me of a food truck in West Philly. Moonlight is walking distance from the house—Camille says, "Right, left, right, you can't miss it." The sun doesn't go down until after 10 p.m. on July nights in Paris. "You can just keep on writing all night," Camille insists.

Moonlight is painted all black and decorated with faux plastic bush grass, faux plastic palm leaves, and faux plastic acacia trees. It's a stereotype of West Africa for Parisians, I assume. I order mouton y riz, a ginger shot, and an ice-cold Cameroonian beer called 33. Sitting there eating with my fingers, I think of my childhood friend, Edmund. He was born in Cameroon. He'd be delighted to see me eating his food. Edmund and I met in the ninth grade, freshman year of high school, on an overnight school trip to the Blue Ridge Mountains.

He was book smart and street smart I called him the king of the code switch. He was the first person I ever met from Africa and even though folks made fun of him for "speaking proper" and having a weird last name and playing soccer, he reminded me of my Trinidadian roots. We were both grounded in a culture and traditions untouched and all its own. Even as a freshman, he declared he was going to the Massachusetts Institute of Technology on a full scholarship when we graduated. His parents were both tenured professors at Hampton University, his mother a scientist and his father a historian. Edmund and I grew to be close friends on that trip; he was laughing at my soccer jokes and challenging me with history lessons and tripping me up on math questions—he was straightforward even when he was wrong. By the end of the trip, we were talking all day and walking through the mountains and even holding hands. I thought as a ninth grader that holding hands meant we'd be together forever, but when we got back from the trip he never said anything that indicated he liked me as anything other than a friend. I was okay with that. Sometimes it's best to keep a good friend a good friend. Edmund was a great friend.

We graduated high school together and I moved to Philly to attend the University of the Arts and he went to MIT as he had planned, but within a year he transferred to Temple University and moved to Philly too to date a girl we both knew from Virginia named Sha. I was hurt for all sorts of reasons, but I understood. Sha was petite and thin, with a large behind, long hair, and a customer service smile. She was at Temple training to be an actress. There was nothing not to like about her besides the fact that everybody wanted a piece of her. I knew her and Edmund would not make it (because true friends know what their friends truly need). She broke his heart and parts of his spirit like I guessed she would. The whole ordeal meant they would never trust each other again. Their breakup broke up our friend group, it was that bad.

We all stopped speaking to one another until one day Edmund saw me hanging out with a group of his street homies at a storefront in North Philly. "I hang with everyone," I tried to explain. I was trying to sublet a corner of their space and start a partnership, but all they wanted to do was smoke weed, drink gin, and listen to Kevin Samuels. It was a small shop on 6th and Girard that they used as a music studio, a skateboard repair place, a weed house, and a screen-printing operation. I was sweeping when through a cloud of thick smoke, Edmund walked in. He'd gotten taller and his shoulders were broad. He looked at me and flipped his wig: "Jeannine?!"

He was shocked and angry.

"Yes?"

"What are you . . . why are you . . . ?"

I started to explain my idea about joining their coworking space to sell books, but he didn't want to hear it.

"This," he pointed and looked around, "is not a coworking space. You are one of the smartest, most creative people around. Does this look like a coworking space to you?"

I looked around. The place was a dump. Someone had built a train track around the perimeter of the store that ran in circles around our heads. But as usual I could only see what I wanted to see and what the space could be with a little love.

"Why would you be in here hanging with losers? This is dumb." The tiny train's horn blared on the word "losers" as it circled around and around my head.

I looked around at everyone and none of his so-called loser friends objected to being called losers. I tried to explain to Edmund that I was going to sublease a piece of their shop and fix it up with the guys, but he only grew more agitated, yelling and slinging the most honest of uplifting quotes.

"You don't see it, do you? You don't even know who you are?

Give me that!" He snatched the broom and turned me around to face a mirror. Breathing hard, chest heaving, hitting the wall and the table as he spoke, he continued, "You are playing small in a too-small universe. Wake up! These guys are losers. They want to use you. They don't love you. Can't you see that?"

Tears came down as I stared at him and myself in the mirror. I was shocked he would say this in a room full of people and not a single person objected. They just continued to pass the blunt like they were watching our conversation play out in a film. I said nothing.

I remembered in ninth grade as we walked through the mountains holding hands that I was taller than Edmund. Now he towered over me as I stared into his eyes. "And I am not going to fall for the tears. Save 'em, Sister. They ain't gonna work here." He paused.

I could not stop the tears if I wanted to. I held my breath to keep from weeping at the disassembling of the fantasy in my head.

"Ok, Pretty Lady. Okay." He handed me a tissue. "I'm sorry this hurts, but you don't belong here."

I thought I was doing fine. Better than ever, I told myself. I just needed somewhere to begin, but you can't just plant seeds on rocky soil and expect them to grow.

"You're fixing up this shithole for these shitty-ass people, Jeannine. And when you are done, they will shit on you. This guy is a weasel and that one a snake and those two are rats and you, my friend, are a soft-ass bunny. Mealtime for scavengers. They will eat you up, spit you out, and pass your bones around as souvenirs." Again no one objected. I couldn't move or speak. I didn't want to believe what he was saying even though it was clear from the silence. "I'm taking you home," he declared. "Right now. Get your things. Let's go."

I cried the entire way home while he continued to lecture me about self-worth. "Jeannine, and I am saying this because I love you, but how did you let Sha (his now ex-girlfriend) write a book before you? How's that even possible?" I shrugged and stared out the window at rowhomes and cement sidewalks. "You deserve bigger and better is all I'm saying—you're dreaming too small."

He held his hand out. "Give me your hand." I listened and held his hand tight for the rest of the car ride.

"Okay," I said when he finally pulled up to my house. Okay was the only word I'd said in over an hour. "Okay. Okay. Okay . . ." He was right.

A few days later one of the losers, the weasel, called me from the shop, and told me not to come in. He said the building had caught on fire in the night. "Maybe it was the crackheads smoking on the roof." His joke was not funny. "The firefighters came quickly, but almost everything was lost to their hoses."

I ran there quickly, only to stare at the front of the destroyed building. I have not seen Edmund ever since. But had it not been for that fire and the fire he lit under me, I may have never moved on to the idea of opening the bookshop on my own; I may have been in a coworking space selling weed and tee shirts and skateboards to this day. But after that conversation, I knew I had to stop hiding or there would be severe consequences—my life would be hell—full of fire and brimstone.

So, sitting in Paris after ten years of not speaking to Edmund, I call him on Facebook from my seat in the back of Moonlight. I take a chance, and he answers. "Hey, Pretty Lady," he says, like we speak every day.

"Hey Ed," I say with a smile. "I am sitting here eating dibi and drinking a 33."

"Why are you in Cameroon?" he laughs.

"Playing soccer," I joke. "No, I'm in Paris."

"For the Olympics?"

"An Olympics all my own. I'm here to write a book. A novel."

"Sweet! Are you gonna tell me about it or do I have to twist your arm?"

"I'm writing . . . a book . . . that's all I can say for now."

"That tracks."

"Yeah, about damn time, right?"

"No time like the present, Jeannine A. Cook," he laughs back. "I see your shops online too. I knew if you could pour all that energy that you were putting into losers into yourself, into your own projects, into what really matters, you could change the world."

The tears start to form. "You there?" he asks.

"I am." I hold a beat. "Edmund, I won't ask if you burnt down that store, I don't want to know." He cracks up. "I just want to say thank you, because you told me the truth that night in a way that I could hear it. Without you, I don't know where I'd be."

"You'd still be in there sweeping up people's shit," he said, poking fun. "Nah, I'm kidding. You were always destined for greatness, Pretty Lady, you were always going to end up right where you are. Sometimes we just need a shove."

"It was a very hard shove."

He snickers. "That's what she said."

We both laugh.

"You just make me so mad; all that potential and you don't

even see it half the time," he continues, before letting the call fall silent. "I almost died a few months ago," he confesses out of the blue. "Last rites and prayers and everything—kidneys failed."

"No way!" I exclaimed. "Like Lazarus?"

"Yeah, it was touch and go for me. I lost so much weight and money and friends. I'm just starting to recover and feel like myself again. Had to stick around for my kid."

"Don't you dare die on us, Ed. I'll never forgive you."

"It wasn't personal," he laughs. Edmund asks about my dad, knowing the history of our tumultuous relationship, and the roller coaster ride of his health.

"He's okay," I lie. "He has a new leg—Lester."

"What?"

"Yeah, he just had his fourth amputation in two years."

"Damn. I'm sorry to hear that."

"Don't be sorry. He's still cracking jokes, he's fine."

"I have another harsh truth to share," Edmund says.

"Not today, Ed. I don't wanna be outside on the streets of Paris weeping."

"You've always been a writer, Jeannine," he says. "Even before the bookshops. You have no choice but to write, deal or no deal, you'll write until the day you die. It's your medicine. Once you begin, you'll never want to stop. If you keep away from weasels, snakes, and rats, you'll be fine. Promise me you'll stay sucker-free," he says.

"Promise," I say, sipping my 33. "I promise, this time."

"Altruism can be a drug, too. And one more thing, Pretty Lady."

"What's that?"

"No matter how far you go, I will always have your back. I'll always hold your hand."

"I know," I tell him sincerely. "I know, Eddie," I repeat in my *Coming to America* accent.

"Love you, friend," he says as the conversation dwindles. "Eat enough dibi for the both of us."

"I love you more," I say, stuffing my face with mouton y riz. "I sure will."

As the days go by, I hang with the waiters at Moonlight night after night. We become quick friends to the point where they start giving me free 33s. They tell me that Paris is sweet for me because of where I am from, but for them, life in Paris is no crystal stair. And like the history of atrocity in the United States that needs to be reckoned with, France has her own work to do on reparation and repair.

My new friends at Moonlight are the Harrietts of this city, not the Josephines. So a bookshop stop on the Overground Underground Railroad is just as necessary here as it is everywhere, I come to believe.

Chapter 29

My phone rings at 2:18 a.m. Paris time. It's Josh—my banker. I've successfully been meeting my daily writing goal for fifteen days straight.

"Jeannine, there's something wrong," Josh says.

"What's new?" I say, disoriented.

"The French embassy is closed."

"And."

"Because of the Olympics."

"And."

"And it's the only place where you can go sign the forms to close on your building. You have to sign on U.S. soil."

"What's this mean, Josh?"

"It means we need to put off your closing until you get back."

"Six weeks. Yeah, that's way too long. The seller will move on. So what now?"

"I don't think you can close, Jeannine. I think we botched this up. I am so sorry; I was so wrong."

Losing this building feels like losing my home. Feels like I'm back in North Philly with crackheads and roaches and families of mice chasing each other across my toes and no toilet and no walls and no heat and no stove. It feels like being arrested by the police for trying to protect someone else's house because you thought you'd be living together but you're living alone. Feels like being beaten then sitting in jail barefoot with bloody feet filled with glass and concrete for trying to stand up to the police. Feels like I'm back in a cell surrounded by other people's spit and pee because sacrificing myself feels right when it comes to protecting a home, even if it's not for me. It feels like dogs on my back and a bounty on my head. It feels like I'm losing the only thing I have. I could escape right now. Give up, stay in Paris, write books, flaneuse, and just never turn back. I don't want to go backward, but sometimes backtracking is the only way forward.

Return and go get it, I hear Ms. Harriett sing like a Sankofa song. Return and go get it.

"I'll come back then," I tell Josh sitting up in my bed with stupid delirium.

"You'll fly 4,000 miles to sign a few pieces of paper?"

"I'll come home from Paris to secure a home for Harriett's." Those are my freedom papers and this has gone on for too long. I've been searching for a building for three years—it's now or never. Without a building the bookshop won't make it. We'll be crushed by the weight of rent, tariffs, and political shifts. The middle-manned nature of bookselling makes it hard to persist.

"Well, if you insist."

I sit silent and still half-asleep; without fight or flight, I'm frozen.

"I do insist."

"And then you'll go back to Paris to finish your novel?" he asks.

"Josh, don't worry about my novel," I laugh.

"Okay, well then, you're closing in two days. See you when you get back."

"Okay, Josh, see you soon. And thanks."

Chapter 30

Of course, I can't go back to sleep. Too much on my mind. I write a note to myself.

Dear Jeannine,

The funny thing about memories is you are never really sure if they exist. Like for the longest you've told yourself the story that once upon a time you walked in on your parents arguing in the garage—this was not unusual. They argued a lot and you needed a clean sock. But this time your mom was down on the floor screaming "stop stop" and your father was standing over her stomping with his boot on her head like her head was made of rocks.

Afterward her eye was swollen and leaking pus. This is how she went completely blind—long-term head trauma to her one good eye.

They'd get back together and break up a thousand million times after, but you don't think she ever forgave him for that.

You don't think he ever forgave himself.

You forgive them both but can't seem to fully remember or fully forget. Did this even happen or is this your childhood imagination playing tricks?

-j

SECTION II:
AUGUST 2024

Jeannine A. Cook interviews Alice Walker

JEANNINE A. COOK: My question is how can we be better sisters to our sisters.

ALICE WALKER: Listen to them even when they say things you don't want to hear.

Chapter 31

The next morning, I fly back to Philadelphia on an Air France three-day round-trip flight. It leaves from Charles de Gaulle instead of Orly. Things are different in this airport, more crowded, more options, more places to get distracted, which makes me late as usual. I am running through Charles de Gualle in heavy leather studded boots, denim shorts, and my colorful knit duster, which keeps snagging on the studs of my boots. I am holding a half-eaten baguette of brie and hot honey. I am the last to board the flight and the most discombobulated. The attendant told me to sit down in the last seat in first class to catch my breath and get myself together rather than shimmy to the back of economy, hitting people in the head with my book bag and baguette. This is my first time in first class. There's a hanger and headphones, a mirror and a mimosa.

I fumble with buttons until I realize my seat can lie completely flat. My cubby door can close. I have privacy like a teeny tiny personal jet. I have a comfy velvet blanket, an eye mask, and white slippers to replace my heavy boots. I fluff my pillow and my phone rings.

"My flight is about to take off. Can't talk."

"I thought you landed days ago."

"I have to come back."

"So soon."

"For three days."

"You buggin'." (Old-school Brooklyn slang.)

"I know."

"Please turn off all electronic devices . . ." the loudspeaker interrupts.

"I gotta fly, Dad."

"You're funny, Number Two."

"I feel funny, Dad."

He laughs. "You're absurd."

I fall asleep before the flight takes off. If I must fly between two cities, I only want to fly like this, with my feet up, my belly full, my wings flat and my mind rested.

After some time, I awaken from a tap on my shoulder and sit up for a three-course meal that includes caviar, haddock, opera cake, and other dishes I can't pronounce.

Best flight ever.

I thank the great mothers for respite when I need it most.

Chapter 32

Dear Ms. Josephine,

Like you, I have two loves. I find myself caught in the middle once again. I feel like Number 2. Do not tell Paris I'm going back to Philly. She can be incredibly sensitive about our time issue. But Ms. Jo, Philly needs me and after all she's been through, I can't let her down. Paris is a new love, so things are still sweet and tender between us. We are still getting to know one another. Who doesn't love the honeymoon phase, but Philly is my ride or die lover, we've been through just about everything. Which is why it's so hard to leave either place. Whenever Philly senses I'm slipping away, she beckons me back to her familiar streets. She has held me my entire adult life, through my toughest moments and for that reason alone, I feel compelled to have her back. Yes, she's a bit rough around the edges, a bit violent, sometimes her attitude stinks, but she means well. I'll be back in Paris before she even notices I've left. Paris will forgive me if she finds out and will continue to love me when I get back, I think. The only one I am neglecting in this love affair is me. It's a tiring ménage à trois, so I'm not sure how much longer I can go on like this—Philly knows my past, Paris knows my future. In Philly I give and in Paris I receive. I need them both. Hold my gray chair at the BNF, hold my seat in Camille's secret jardin, hold my place at Moonlight. If Paris asks, tell her I won't be gone long. It's only three days, but when I get back I'll have officially tied the knot with Philly.

 That's just between us. Don't say a thing.

 I promise to write.

Much love,

-j

Chapter 33

When I land, I decide I will use the next three days to complete the renovation on the bookshop, buy our building, and visit Lorene Cary's archive at the Rosenbach Library. But sometimes the great mothers mess with my plans. Just when I begin to settle into my Society Hill apartment, I get a call from my good sister-cousin-auntie friend, Sannii.

"Evenin' Sugah," Sannii says in a Southern drawl. She has Southern sensibilities that remind me of my neighbors back down South in Virginia. She is my chosen family in Philadelphia, since otherwise I have none. In my neighborhood, Tidemill, folks used to greet each other with a good morning, a nice to see you, a hey how ya been. I grew up in a neighborhood where my neighbors were friends. Even though Sannii is from the Nicetown section of North Philly, and her family has been in North Philly for generations, she reminds me that we are from a tradition of neighbors with no specific geographical location. Love is our common language.

"Hey hey, Honey Honey," I say in a Southern drawl.

"It's time, Sugah," she whispers.

I know what that means. Sannii and I have had a standing-in-the-gap tea date for as long as I can remember. At least once a month we meet up for a tea and honey break. For almost a decade she has been the creative doula who uses teas and honeys to help me deliver my offspring. She speaks in metaphors of machetes and roses, razor blades and hand grenades.

"I thought I had more time," I plead.

I have a laundry list of things to do over the next three days that don't involve sitting down drinking tea.

Complete the paint job

Hang the light fixtures

Hang the shelves

Arrange the books

Get more books

Clear the space of the mounds and mounds of dust that construction brings

Close on the building

Hire a videographer to record me closing on the building

Visit the Rosenbach

Fish through Lorene Cary's archives at the Rosenbach

Write my questions for Lorene Cary interview.

Get back to the airport

Get back to Paris

Get back to writing

Complete novel

But Sannii insists, "Sugah, you can't give birth while flying a plane." It's time for us to go down by the riverside where mothers have given birth for centuries. She'll bring the honey (rosemary infused) and the tea leaves (mint—my favorite). All I have to do is bring me.

I am not in the mood, but I say, "Okay."

Sannii is not the kind of cousin-sister-auntie friend who you turn down when she requests teatime. And if you do, she'll likely say in the sweetest form of pretty poetry, "Oh, yes you do have time for you."

"Okay."

I call Unc to paint so I can take a break. I've been working with him for years; he's the only person who came with me from the shop on 6th and Girard that caught fire and he remains with me to this very day. He's done construction on every one of my bookshop renovations except Paris because he's too afraid to fly. Unc is a self-proclaimed man of the juice and makes me laugh and cry. I tried to hire a professional construction crew, because Unc is slower and older than he used to be, and I can tell when he works now that his knees are in pain. But my plan backfires and I end up having to call Unc anyway. He wants a Natty Ice and a pack of Newport Lights, and he will get the place painted in a day. "Gotta hit it with the Killz," he says. I ask him if he's coming with me back to Paris. He tells me only if I'm driving there because he ain't getting on nobody's plane. "What do I look like, a bird?"

"Unc, you don't have to be a bird to have wings. Fly, Eagles, fly," I sing.

In Philly, Unc is the closest thing I have to a father because he always comes to my rescue and saves the day.

I also call Harvey, who I met one morning at 7 a.m. in

Home Depot while we both searched for paint. I was singing and excited, as I always am in Home Depot, getting ready to change the bookshop with Unc. I'm singing Tammi Terrell's part of "Ain't no mountain high enough, ain't no river wide enough . . ." when this young man asks me if I am singing to him. I tell him "I'd only sing to my love, like Tammi did Marvin Gaye."

He says, "Well, then I'll be your love."

He tells me I'll need his phone number since we are lovers now. I go to put his number into my phone, and I already have his number and his name saved, Harvey.

"Are you the CIA, Harvey?" I ask with a customer service smile.

"Call me later and I'll remind you how we know each other, my love."

That's steamy, I think. *And scary.*

Over dinner, I learn that I met Harvey the last time I was in Paris. It's a long story that will have its own book, but long story short, we met but I never saw him. He was born and raised in Philly, albeit upper middle class, private school, Mt. Airy Philly. He doesn't scare easily. He doesn't like to get his hands dirty, but he agrees to get his hands dirty for me. Turns out Harvey is the grandson of Judge Harvey Schmidt whose book collection we've inherited. He provides Unc with a steady supply of Natty Ice and cigarettes and to my surprise he also agrees to help Unc paint while I go for a walk with my sister-cousin-auntie friend.

"I'll be your muse," he tells me. "For the love interests in your books."

"That's what everyone says," I laugh and say, "Okay."

Harvey asks where I am heading but he wouldn't understand, so I say, "I have a standing tea date with my good sister-cousin-auntie friend—Sannii."

"Remember the day I set you free. I told you you could always count on me darling. . . . When will you be back?" he asks. Then goes back to singing our song.

"I'll be back first thing in the morning, if the creek don't rise."

"What creek?" He's serious and millennial and Northern. (It's old Southern slang, Harvey!)

"I'm going to Tacony," I laugh.

Sannii commends me on finding help and a lover who is willing to paint. She says, "I'll meet you down by the riverside in an hour."

I arrive late as usual because I drive extra slowly. She's sitting in her car waiting for me at the mouth of the long green passageway of woodlands and meadows and wildflowers that is Tacony Creek Park—a 300-acre watershed preserve that runs alongside an ever-flowing and sometimes overflowing creek. As we begin down the path laughing and catching up as old friends do, the clear bright sky turns black and blue.

Sannii is almost always in sneakers, jeans, and a fitted baseball cap. No one would suspect she passes down ancient wisdom and remedies. She blends in well for a sage, I tell her.

"Chile, I'm from Norf Philly," she reminds me when I ask her what realm she's really from. "Norf! Where we keep razorblades under our tongues and roses between our toes." That sounds painful, I think (and otherworldly). I wonder if she's speaking in metaphor or the real thing. Neither would surprise me with Sannii.

I have on a thin white flowy dress intended for flouncing around during my final days in France, but instead I'm wearing it in Philly with my leather studded boots, which I decide go with everything, and a vintage denim newsboy cap. Because denim goes with everything too. Sannii is always prepared with a tote bag full of ingredients and I always am not. I don't even have a bag.

"You see this wind," she begins, as the sycamores dance and wave at us from both sides of the trail.

"Hard to miss it," I say, holding onto my hat.

"She's here."

"Who is she?"

"She who speaks on the wind."

"That's how the mothers speak to me, too," I tell Sannii. But my dress is white and paper thin; it'll be see-through if it gets wet. That would be a sight for sore eyes. It's gonna rain. "Should we head back?"

Bikers and joggers make haste toward their cars and away from the river. "It's gonna pour!" one of the joggers exclaims as he runs the opposite way.

Sannii smiles and waves him off. "No, Sugah, she is sending them off *your* path. Preparing a place for *you*. Indeed, water will break, but the rain will hold back," Sannii tells me as we forge ahead.

"Thank goodness for these boots," I tell her. They can withstand anything.

As we arrive at a bend in the path, the widest part of the creek appears before us.

"Here?" she asks.

"Not sure."

"Okay, then it's not here because you'll know for sure where you want to give birth."

We walk ahead some more though I am only pregnant with an idea. We find shaded shallow area where we can see the redbreast and bluegills swimming past the rocks.

I don't want to give birth right now; I want to finish my laundry list. "Too much talking and not enough listening will put you in an early grave. It's time to push this thing out. Birth her, Sugah. You, she, I, we, us deserve every sweet thing. What you've been feeling are contractions, but today if you want to fully birth your new self, you must declare it out loud before it rains."

We stand at the edge of the rocks and the raging creek. Sannii pulls a jar of honey and a spoon out from her bag. She instructs me to put the honey on my tongue three times and remind myself out loud that I deserve sweetness. "Say it."

"I deserve sweetness," I say, putting a teensy tiny bit of honey on my tongue too fast.

"You deserve more than that, Sugah. Slow down. Concentrate. Say it like you mean it 'cause you mean it."

I fill up my spoon with honey and swallow it down in one gulp.

"I deserve sweetness," I repeat smacking my lips together.

The storm clouds grow thicker, the wind more intense, the creek more ravenous. Moisture is in the air.

"Many have gathered here for your birthing," she laughs at the clouds and trees. "It's a joyous occasion."

I smile as the thick rosemary-infused honey coats my throat and my stomach.

"So, what sweetness would you like to give birth to next?

Whisper it in the wind, Sugah, and pour a bit of honey into the creek afterward."

I pause. Take in the rushing water, the rocks, the rushing clouds, and the rushing wind. "I'd like to taste the sweetness of love," I giggle.

"And so it is. You will write your own love story." She stands stoic and bowlegged with her hands on her hips braced against the wind. "What else, Sugah. Push."

"I'd like to taste the sweetness of . . . the land." I drip a bit of honey on my tongue. "Because the land deserves to be returned to us, and us to it." I don't know where that comes from, but before I can think about it long, I've already said it and Sannii has moved on.

"Whoa, Sugah. You can say that again."

She waits as if something is speaking to her. Holds her hand up to make me stand still. "Before you make this last push, take a deep breath in and look at me."

I look at Sannii and wonder where she learned these things. How she knows what she knows. Where is she from? Norf Philly, but it's like ancient wisdom lives in her loins. Her gifts, she calls them machetes, give her the ability to cut through things. And if you're lucky she will loan you a sword.

"I come from women who like sharp objects," she told me once before I birthed the bookshop. For a month before I opened Harriett's Bookshop, Sannii came weekly, every Tuesday, and sat with me in the near-empty space to share a cup of tea. Every week she'd ask me if I was ready to open my doors and every week, I had another excuse why I wasn't ready. "I don't have enough of this . . . I am waiting until I have more of that." Until one Tuesday we were sitting there sipping our tea and laughing, when a man walked in and started to browse right in front of our faces. I didn't realize I'd left the door unlocked. Just when I was about to tell him, "We are not quite open yet," Sannii placed her hand on my shoulder and said, "Breathe, Sugah. This is happening." That day we sold our first book, *Parable of the Sower* by Octavia Butler. I told the customer I didn't have a cash register yet, and he said, "Keep the change," while walking out, already reading.

"I'd like to taste the sweetness of . . . a sweet life." I pour more honey in the river and drip a bit more on my tongue. I close my eyes, feel the wind, and let out a deep sigh—a silent guttural exhale.

"And so it is," she says, pouring the remaining honey in the river and watching the tail of the residue sail off into the wind. "And so it is," she repeats giving me a high five.

"And so it is," I repeat.

Next Sannii pulls yellow flowers and green herbs and brown teas from her tote bag. I'm thinking, *Oh now we are for sure gonna get caught in this rain. I didn't think we were actually drinking tea out here, too.* She instructs me to pour each item into the creek a little at a time. The yellow flowers and green herbs and brown teas float away. Then she gives me apples and a bit of rum. I do as instructed. "Let the river have her way," she tells me, "you're ready for every sweet thing."

I agree with a head nod. We hum our way back to the main road in a slow saunter of softness unencumbered by the impending rain. The sky grows mighty dark, and the wind grows mighty strong. Yet it doesn't affect our walk at all. When we both get into our cars, a few drops hit the windshield, and then the sky explodes. I sit still in the storm and text another chapter of *It's Me They Follow* into my phone. This is how the sweetness mantra became central to the novel. As the main character repeats the spell, "I deserve sweetness," over and over again to herself, she reminds me and you to do the same.

"Thank you, Honey, Honey," I text to Sannii's phone.

"You're welcome, Sugah."

Chapter 34

The next morning, I wake up before the sun. *It's closing day*, but the world is opening up. I lie still on my paisley vintage couch. It is one of only four pieces of furniture in my Society Hill apartment. I bought it from a garage sale in South Jersey on a farm in Cherry Hill with pygmy horses and a white picket fence. Facebook Marketplace bookhunting has taken me to meet many amazing people, places, and things. I get to the farm to buy books and see a couch I love and end up spending the day and then many months getting to know the woman who sells to me. She is an artist and author with breast cancer who is having chemo and selling books and furniture to pay her medical bills. Her farm becomes another one of my special places and her couch reminds me of that farm. Her couch is where I sleep, eat, write, and have conversations with Ms. Harriett.

This morning, like most mornings, I am awakened on the couch by a flock of birds that seem to follow me. All I hear is a fury of chirps that sound less like singing and more like milieu. *Maybe they are excited*, I think. Maybe they are feeding off my energy. I feel like it's my wedding day. I have butterflies in my stomach; my heart is going at its usual extra fast speed. I check my hands, no trembles, that means I am okay, but I can't seem to hold a thought for too long—they rush over me like hot springs.

I finally grip one and hold it tight. It's a scene from three years ago—summer of 2021. I was working in the bookshop late at night. Tinkering in silence while setting up for the next day, when I got an email that requires a trigger warning. Continue at your own risk or flip to the next chapter. It read,

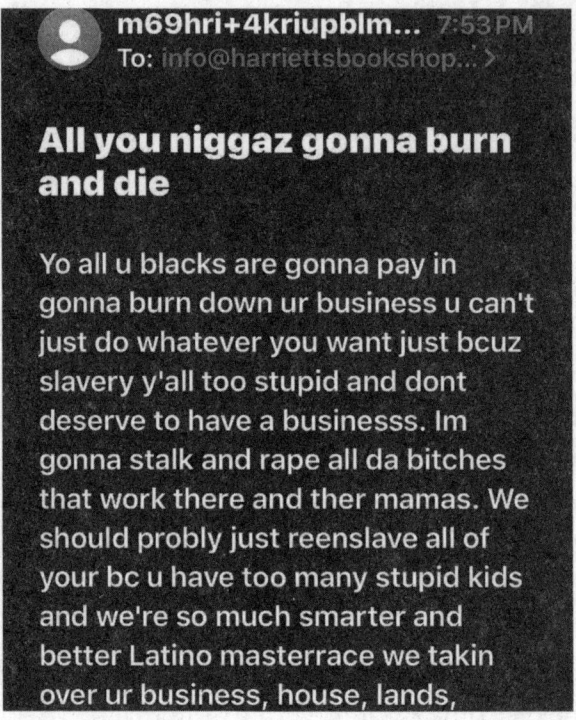

What in the hell, I thought as I put my phone down. What in the fuck? I picked my phone back up to see if what I was reading was what I thought. "Rape all da bitches," and I looked up and there was a man standing outside of the shop looking in. What in the hell, I started to say. But I stopped myself. I'll never know whether he was just an innocent book lover peeking in at his favorite titles or someone more nefarious and sinister. What in the hell. I slipped behind the wall in the children's room of the bookshop, to hide out until the man walked away. I looked at the email again to see if it was spam, but it grew ever more heinous as I read on, and like any coward, the sender didn't sign a name.

I never thought about how dangerous opening a tiny 500-square-foot bookshop could be. I thought Harriett's would be a safe place for creative introverts to hang out quietly together.

But at that time, summer 2021, George Floyd had been murdered, Breonna Taylor was dead, people were isolated and angry, anxious and afraid, there was a cloud of dread, and I was flying around giving out free books at protests because that was all I had to give. Storefront windows were being bashed in. Protesters were gathering and counter-protesters were gathering. It was like fire and brimstone.

In the neighborhood over from mine in Port Richmond, an entire shopping center was set ablaze and broken into and left in disarray. I was flying in and out of town with suitcases full of books on near-empty planes. Every time I went to a different city, something wild happened in Philadelphia as "that energy" crept closer and closer.

While I was in Minneapolis giving out Malcolm X books, news was erupting of bat-wielding Fishtowners yelling slurs and marching directly in front of Harriett's. I cut my trip short and when I flew back, I started sleeping at the bookshop because I read somewhere that people are less likely to bash the windows of a business if they see someone inside, so I was inside with the lights on all day and all night, thinking *Over my dead body will some coward with a bat and bad language take this bookshop away.*

But the night when I got the email, I realized I needed an actual plan, not just big energy and strong affirmations—I needed strategy. Like what would I do if someone actually broke in? I created two routes out the back way.

What would I do if they bashed my windows? Glass fragments in the head can cause deep lacerations and irreparable damage to the brain. I think of Malcolm X in his 1965 speech, "After the Firebombing," saying, "I was in a house last night that was bombed, it was my own." What would I do if someone grabbed me on my way to my car and tried to rape me? What about the youth conductors who were working for me? What about their safety? And the safety of my customers? I spiraled. Up until then, to survive the pandemic, we would build a bookshop outside on the corner. We would take all of the shelves, all of the props, all of the plants, all of the books outside and lock the door with a note that said, "Books for sale on honor system with our Cash App and Venmo." We were doing everything we could think of to keep our heads above water and help others do the same. The answer is books, I told myself every morning when I woke up. Stories preserve humanity.

But now here I was in my own bookshop, unclear whether the man standing in my storefront window was there to kidnap me, bust open my windows, or just browse through my display.

I called Lazarus. "Dad, what if someone tries to kill me?" I asked as I stood behind the children's book room wall and peeked at the man in the window.

"You kill them back," he joked.

"Dad, I am serious. I just got an email. The person said . . . well they said a lot of things. But one thing was, I'm gonna kill you."

"Where are you?"

"The shop."

"With who?"

"Ms. Harriett."

"It's three in the morning, Number 2. You buggin' talking about you in the shop with Ms. Harriett. You and Ms. Harriett have any weapons in there?"

"Just an old Harriett Tubman era axe."

"You need an old Harriett Tubman era rifle."

"Dad, I'm serious."

"Me too," he laughed. "Trust your instincts. When I was in the army . . ."

I didn't want to hear another army story.

"Dad . . ." I rolled my eyes and took the phone from my ear.

"Do you want me to call the police?" I heard him say after I was silent for too long.

"The police who killed Breonna Taylor, Dad? Or the ones who killed George Floyd? Which ones will respond to your call? How do you know which ones will show up and see me in here with this axe? And not think I'm target practice. Nah, Dad. Hard pass."

"I'll stay on the phone with you, then."

"Oh and there's a man outside." I peeked and the man in the window was still there.

"What kind of man, Jeannine?" When he gets mad my dad speaks at a high pitch.

"I don't know, Dad. He has on a tee shirt and a Phillies cap."

"Jeannine. You are supposed to be a reader and a writer, and you can't come up with a better description of the man than that?" he laughed.

I laughed too.

"I think he's looking at books."

"At three in the morning?"

"Well, I do have the lights on."

"Okay, that's plausible."

"If he were trying to kill you, he's the slowest murderer. Prob a reader."

"Dad!"

"Just saying."

"Dad, what are you doing up anyway?"

"Couldn't sleep, I was in pain."

"What kinda pain?"

"The kind that hurts. That kind of pain . . ."

"I was just . . ."

"Remember that time when the Phillies won the World Series back in 2008?" he laughed and changed the subject.

"Dad, you're an awful listener, but yeah, I remember."

"Was it their first one or something?"

"Not the first but . . ."

"I can't remember . . . I follow the Mets, not the Phillies. But anyway, remember how Philly erupted. Remember that?"

"Yes, Dad, but what does this have to do with someone threatening to kill me?"

"And folks were climbing poles and partying in the streets and cheering so loud we could hear them from Virginia?"

"Yeah."

"Just think about that."

"Think about what?"

"That night. It was crazy. And when your city won that night—four games to one—it was quite the game and everyone came together."

"Dad, how do you remember that?"

"All I'm saying is you know a lot about a city by how they

love their sports teams. Your city has a lot of love in it. Don't let anyone tell you different. You live in a city with a lot of love. Plus, you was really born in Brooklyn, so you got that Brooklyn spirit too. Yeah, it took forever for you to come out. I just knew you was gonna be a boy. My junior. Everywhere we went old ladies were coming up to your mother while she was pregnant with you saying like, 'Oh yup up we can tell by the way she is carrying, that right there, that's gonna be your boy.' And then after you made me wait like twenty-eight hours, you come out a girl. And I was like 'ahh damn.'"

"What, Dad? You delirious or something? You skipping from the Phillies to my birth story?"

"All I'm saying, Number 2, is you'll be fine. Don't believe the hype."

And then the man outside of my window walked off.

"Okay, Dad. He walked away."

My dad stayed on the phone talking about sports teams coming back to play. And the Special Olympics being canceled. "Man, that's messed up, man."

I was tired, but I couldn't cut him off after he'd stayed up with me. Also, it was good to have someone on the other line in case the mystery man came back. Then Lazarus went from sports to politics. "These were the first riots and they won't be the last. Just these idiots burning down their own neighborhoods, that never made no sense to me."

"But Dad, what about riots being the language of the unheard?"

"Sometimes when you're not being hear, you should just shut up and do your own thing. What's the message right now? What's the demand? How will you know you've made change if you don't even know what you want in the first place? They'll pacify you with trinkets to calm the noise and when everything is back to normal, they'll snatch all your toys. We've seen this before. It repeats in history, from Reconstruction to Rodney King. You were young, but you were alive—you should remember Rodney King. They get mad, they burn everything down and then go back to business as usual in a few days."

"You don't think it'll be different this time? It's record-breaking numbers of people in the streets."

"I think history repeats itself in the worst possible way. At least you handing out books. That's history repeating itself too, though. At least those books will outlast the rage, long as someone uses the books for more than shelf decoration."

"I'm getting sleepy," I said, still gripping that old Harriett Tubman era axe.

"Good, 'cause I'm tired as hell."

"Night, Dad! Or good morning!" The sun was coming up. The birds chirping and singing in milieu.

"Night, Jeannine. Now go home and get some rest. Tomorrow's another day."

I said okay, but I could not relax after that. I screenshotted the email and posted it that morning for the world to see with a caption that read, "This is the bullshit small businesses have to go through just trying to make it out here—which is why we need to protect and serve one another."

The post went viral with thousands of shares, hundreds of comments, and my video had more views than I care to count. Calls started flooding in. Calls from the Omega Psi Phi Fraternity who were coming to stand watch, calls from the Fruit of Islam, who was coming when the others couldn't be there. I even got a call from Lorene who had a group of granny friends who said, "We will come and walk you to your car." Like a grandmothers' brigade. Friends near and far sent love in the form of flowers and bottled water and candles and letters to the bookshop for days, even though it was the thick of COVID and we had been instructed to stand six feet apart. We stood together in other ways. Someone even bought me a machete and left it out front still in the package with a note: "Read up on the history of the machete." Neighbors made plans of signals I could send if I were ever in distress. A doctor who just purchased a forty-acre farm called and said, "Girl, if you ever need safe passage, I got all this land and a lot of guns." Love was flying in from everywhere. This is the Overground Underground Railroad, I told Ms. Harriett—it's two hundred years later but the spirit is the same because it travels through time and space.

Then two investigators showed up one day as I was locking up. They were sitting outside for I don't know how long in an unmarked vehicle watching the shop. They hopped up and walked over kind of strange.

"Jeannine?" one said.

"Yes." He startled me. "We saw your post," he said, handing me his card.

"Yeah."

"Well, what happened?"

I repeated the story you've just read.

"Why didn't you call the police? The district is right up the street."

"Breonna Taylor."

"Excuse me?" the officer said.

"People call the police and end up dead. I didn't call the police; I called the people."

"We wanted you to know we are taking this seriously and there's an active investigation on the threats. It seems several other small businesses in the area received similar messages."

"Okay, well, thank you."

"Contact me if you need anything."

And I think that is what took me over the edge, that and lack of sleep. It's one thing to have someone threatening me, but to have someone threatening a whole group of us just wouldn't leave my head.

As the investigators drove away, I turned on my camera phone, which I really hate doing, but something had to be said. Saying in a few weeks we would be shutting down Girard Ave. and hosting a modern-day sit-in. I was upset and tired and inspired, and I needed other people like me to gather and connect because things were starting to get insane.

"We are hosting a modern-day sit-in," I repeated.

After I posted that video, I realized I had no idea what a modern-day sit-in was.

Perhaps that was another message from Ms. Harriett. When I am having a Conversation with Ms. Harriett they mostly come in the mornings, a slew of random unannounced ideas drops into my head like rain. I call it a download because it feels like I am an old computer, and she has inserted a USB drive full of information into my head, and then I am flooded with visions and understandings and questions and flashbacks for minutes or hours or days. Then I must research to understand all the new thoughts. The thought of owning my building and delivering books on horseback came in as a part of a larger download when I was trying to understand what a modern-day sit-in would look like. It came in along with thoughts about sharecropping and land rights, and the Garifuna and the Geechee and the Maroons and the Lenape, about John Seward and John Tubman and Johnny Appleseed. Suddenly, I knew that renting my space during times of mass uncertainty was unsustainable and unsafe. Businesses were closing all around me because they didn't own the spaces where they stayed, and now we were under direct threat from a nameless, faceless thing. If we didn't do something quick, we were sure to be washed away.

So, although I wanted to scurry into the tiniest hole, put a cover over my head, Ms. Harriett whispered during our conversation like a general in the back of my brain, "I have heard their groans and sighs and seen their tears and I would give every drop of blood in my veins to free them. We do not run or hide. You know what we have to do, right?"

"No, I don't!" I exclaimed (in the back of my head).

"Buy a building," she repeated. "If you want to protect and serve your people, plant your roots into the ground so when mighty winds come, you won't be blown away. Be here for them. Be here with them. Be a source of nutrients in the soil and let it spread through their veins."

"Nutrients in the soil?! During COVID? With barely any money selling books on the honor system, having owned nothing before but debt from degrees and every adversity in the world against me—literal threats on my life—you expect me now to figure out how to buy a building? How, Ms. Harriett?" I thought, like I was talking to Sway.

She's a general and she doesn't like a lot of back talk. She went silent, but as usual she was right.

So, after a minute I simply said, "Okay."

Three years later, on August 15, 2024, I wake on closing day, ready to open my world. I feel like I am getting married because this is the ultimate commitment.

"Today, I buy your building," I say to Ms. Harriett. "Just like you said."

The birds chirp even louder and the sunlight creeps in.

I run to the bathroom to get ready, but I forget one thing.

Chapter 35

This essay was written alongside the youth conductors who helped me distribute books to protesters in Louisville, Minneapolis, and Philly during the Uprising. It was commissioned for the anthology *How We Stay Free*, edited by Christopher Rogers, Fajr Muhammad, Michael Jared Lowe and the Paul Robeson House and Museum.

The Greatest Love of All: A Counterattack

"We are under attack," I am reminded when my sister-friend sends me a link to a news article about a young Breonna Taylor's murder. It is a hot gray morning in May of 2020. Multiple people have shared the story with me at this point. "She was in bed, Jeannine," my older sister says and repeats through sobs. "Sleeping, I know. I know," I need a distraction. Music will help me. Whitney Houston plays on the radio singing "The Greatest Love of All." Which only makes me feel worse. I turned it off. A year later and I still feel grief for Breonna in waves. Mostly in the mornings. A feeling that grips at the backs of my eye sockets. I am plotting out mood settling techniques. Naturally, I am mourning, but not consciously, it is a more deep-in-my-spirit type mourning, a heaviness like fatty deposits that lives in my blood vessels. It does not stay, but when it hits, it is an attack. "We are under attack," I type in the notes section of my phone.

I am a shopkeeper at Harriett's, an independent bookstore in the Fishtown section of Philadelphia. In the shop, I train groups of Youth Conductors, what I lovingly call our interns, to be community leaders under the guiding light of Harriett Tubman. Most of our Youth Conductors are girls. Tell me, how do you listen to the confusion and sadness in a young girl's voice when she shares her version of Breonna Taylor's life story with you? When do you explain state-sanctioned lynching to this dear child? How do you put this murder into a historical perspective? When do you tell her that she is under attack?

"You give her an outlet," Ms. Harriett whispers in my left ear. "Don't be afraid to take her to the frontlines and let her be heard," the ancient voice says in my subconscious mind. So, I do. I'd gone to Minneapolis to give out books to organizers protesting the murder of George Floyd a few weeks earlier. We'd given out books here on the streets of Philadelphia. It felt completely imbalanced not to travel to Louisville to do something on behalf of Breonna Taylor. I took the Youth Conductors with me. We flew to Kentucky to read to children in Injustice Park and distribute free books to parents. Instead, when we arrived, we were surrounded by militarized police officers and snipers on roofs. Of course, storytime was canceled, but our mission to celebrate women authors, artists, and activists continued. We gave away all we had. Our Youth Conductors stood in front of hundreds of organizers, protestors, and police chanting "free books" and "Knowledge is power" as they handed out copies of The Organizing Skills Guide written by my friend and mentor Daniel Hunter. We gave away everything we had, and when the Youth Conductors were ready, we left. That night we sat silent, listening to shootings outside. We found out later that one person was killed, and multiple people were injured there in the park a few hours after we'd left. "We are still under attack," I say to myself on the plane leaving Kentucky.

"We went to a protest for the death of Breonna Taylor in Louisville KY. At the protest, when we first got there, we saw a bunch of cops with huge guns looking at everyone. The whole thing was divided with the cops in the streets at a gate, almost as if they were trying to hold back the protesters. I was scared to walk in the streets because of the police, but me and Bri got the books and we passed them out to each and every person. Everyone there was so kind and thankful for the pins and books we gave out. Being at the protest I learned the importance of fighting for a cause in spite of people that stand in your way."—Jen, Harriett's Youth Conductor, age 12

It's been a year since our visit to Louisville, and I am sitting outside under the rays of a new spring sun, thinking about what to write for this submission, and the song, "The Greatest Love of All" by Whitney Houston comes on again. And, sure maybe it was a coincidence, but I take in the lyrics this time. That same ancient voice that I call Ms. Harriett says once again, "You give them an outlet." So here at the frontlines of this essay are the youth's words as an outlet and another chance for them to lead the way. And while I am humming the lyrics to the song, it occurs to me just what happened to Whitney Houston. And what it means to lose a Sister so publicly. And how many of us mourned Whitney and how many of us still do. What does it mean to exalt our sisters' names in their deaths and how do we memorialize their legacy for generations to come? This woman gave society, our culture, many cultures, all she had, and all the Youth Conductors know about is her tragic death. So, I play "The Greatest Love of All" for them on repeat and sing the lyrics aloud to remind them that they are loved. I text them the lyrics and ask them to memorize them so they, too, can sing along.

"Going to Louisville, Kentucky, was one of the most remarkable experiences that I've ever encountered. Being that Louisville was my first time ever going to the South, it was definitely a culture shock. Everything from the food, the people, and the environment gave me a new perspective. Walking into the protest, I could feel a different energy. The police stood in formation on the street, firearms in hands, ready for anything as the civilians stood and chanted closer to the sidewalk. There were countless signs along the curb vocalizing the frustration felt in the air.

"When I first heard about Breonna Taylor, I was nauseated. The fact that people could do such a thing with no reason or remorse was appalling to me. Standing in the exact place where Breonna Taylor was blatantly murdered only made me realize the power that we have. The impact that we can make on the system and the influence that we hold over our brothers and sisters. Only then did I truly comprehend my role in the many protests that I've participated in as a Harriett's Bookshop Youth Conductor. We must educate ourselves and share the knowledge that is bestowed upon us. We must use these times as an opportunity to better ourselves and the next generation. As I learn that STILL, no one is being held accountable for Breonna Taylor's death, it only makes me want to fight more." —Bri, Harriett's Youth Conductor, age 17

"Greatest Love of All" was written by a woman named Linda Creed from right here in Philadelphia. She wrote the song on her deathbed as she was battling breast cancer. She attended Germantown High School and penned multiple classics for the Sound of Philadelphia. I tell the Youth Conductors that the song's Philly roots explain its raw realness. Linda died just before the release and major success of Whitney Houston's rendition of her song. But my dear Linda, your legacy lives on. And then this verse reminds me of Breonna Taylor and about the current state of activism. And about state-sanctioned lynching. And about the co-opting of movements. And I imagine what it would look like if we dedicated time to mourn and repair harm properly. And I remember the first day that I told the Youth Conductors to take to the streets with books instead of signs that read "I Can't Breathe." And how we went back and forth about it, but in the end, they listened to me, and now we've distributed a few thousand books. All because that is all that we had. And how sometimes we find ourselves seeking a hero to do activism on our behalf when in reality, we are the only ones who can fulfill our needs.

"As an intern at Harriett's Bookshop, I am educated and aware of what is needed of me in order to alter the world and create a social change. I am a biracial female born in a Latin household. Prior to being an intern, I was insecure of the African features bestowed upon me. I desired the Latin features that were concealed. When discussing this problem with Jeannine and participating in the various events at the bookshop, I gained an understanding that African features are something to display with confidence. Through understanding this, I was capable of advocating for a social change because I knew that I was not the only biracial female who felt this way. Society targets anything associated with African Americans, and Harriett's allowed me to understand that. On another occasion, a song titled "Can't Breathe" was presented to the 9/10 Choir at my school. The song focused on the issue of police brutality towards the minority, but it was in the perspective of the minority. The majority of the 9/10 Choir is of European descent, resulting in me feeling uncomfortable to hear people who do not deal with these hardships state "I Can't Breathe." I felt disgusted. When I informed Harriett's team of this problem, I felt supported. They were informed on how to deal with this disagreement. I discussed the issue with a choir teacher and after a few months, the song was removed from the 9/10 Choir. Society attempts to ensure that people of African descent are quiet, but I will not please society's expectations of me. As a Youth Conductor, I am no longer silenced. I have gained a different perspective of being a person of African descent. I will continue to advocate and fight for a change." —Ye Ye, Harriett's Youth Conductor, age 16

Finally, to the Youth Conductors, who boldly stood on the frontlines of many protests beside me, who follow in Harriett's footsteps beside me, and whose words live on in this anthology beside mine, remember that even though we are still under attack, you are the greatest counterattack. You have the right and the responsibility to lead the way, to live as you believe, and to find your strength in love. Ase.

Chapter 36

I arrive at Tioga Franklin Bank to close on our building and realize I forgot to put on deodorant. I'm sweating like a hog. (I know hogs don't sweat, Harvey! It's Southern slang.) It's a ninety-degree August day. I search for deodorant in my bag but don't find any. I am waiting for the bank president and other fancy bank executives to arrive, and I'm scared when they walk in it will smell like my bad nerves. I've invited a cameraman to come with me to capture this momentous occasion.

"What should I capture?" he asks when he arrives.

"Capture everything. So I can show my great-great-great-grandchildren one day."

He is watching my every move like paparazzi and now I wish I never invited him. I am sure he is capturing me subtly trying to sniff myself and look for any good-smelling thing in my oversized bag. But as usual I am not quite as prepared as I wish I were. I get up to go to the restroom and he gets up to follow me.

"No, I'm okay." I give him a stop hand while trying not to raise my arms too high.

"Gotcha, you told me to capture everything, so . . ."

"Not everything," I say, rushing off.

I run into the restroom, and indeed it is me who is not only sweating profusely but starting to smell. I am sweating from excitement and nervousness and fear and accomplishment and perseverance and all the things life serves me—including interminable heat. There is soap in the bank bathroom, but it is unscented. I make a washcloth out of paper towel and give myself a bird bath, trying my best to wash any odor away. I rub more soap under my arms, hoping it will keep me from sweating and the smell from coming again.

I look at myself in the mirror and laugh. What's the point in looking good, when you smell this way? My mother would kill me if she were here. She spent so many years of her life navigating using her nose. A nice breeze comes in through the floor vent air conditioner, so I hold my arms up over the vent and try to dry my sweat. I laugh and wonder if Ms. Harriett gets a kick out of watching me do this type of stuff. Big things are easy for me, but small things are hard. Like even though I was nervous about raising the money to buy the building, that was fairly easy. But remembering to pack an extra deodorant on a 93-degree day—hard.

We raised $75,000 the first weekend we launched our Home for Harriett's fundraising campaign. All I did was post a message and send a newsletter out declaring, "We need a permanent home for Harriett's before it is too late," and voilà! We would raise double that in three months and then I'd spend three years learning how commercial real estate works in Philadelphia. Lots of learning, only to end up right where we started, in the building we were in the entire time—buying 258 E. Girard Avenue.

How could I get us this far and forget something so minor, yet so important, as deodorant, on such an important day?

I stuff paper towels under both of my underarms and hope they soak up the sweat and smell. I open the door, and the cameraman is waiting there with his lens in my face ready to go. He follows me into the boardroom where the once-empty table is now filled with executives in suits, including the president of the bank, Dr. Terry McEwen.

One day, just when I was telling Ms. Harriett that I couldn't figure this out, Terry walked into the bookshop and said, "I am the president of Tioga Franklin Bank, literally a few doors down from the bookshop, and we want to work with you."

"Terry, I need y'all to hold my hand through the entire process. Okay?"

"We got you, Jeannine. Whatever you need."

He has kept that promise to this very day.

On the flip side, there was another lending organization who announced publicly that they were working with us at a huge community event (I guess for kudos or clout), but when it came time to purchase the building, they were nowhere to be found. The right people always come, and the wrong people end up disappearing. Remember neglect can be your ally.

Closing on a building is extra boring, and I feel bad for the videographer because for me the process is like watching paint dry. But he is excited and films like he's watching the Olympic games.

I make a story in my head for the novel. I laugh at the idea of The Shopkeeper trying to attend writing class without any deodorant on. It is this moment that inspired the scene in the novel where The Shopkeeper shows up to her writing group with her underarms smelling rank.

I sign what feels like hundreds of papers with my arms stuck close to my sides like a tyrannosaurus for almost an hour. The paper towel is working, and I don't know if everyone is being extra professional or if anyone besides the nosy cameraman suspects a thing. When we are done everyone stands up to shake hands and congratulate me. I awkwardly maneuver from person to person, but when I get too close to the president, Terry, I lose control of myself, lifting my arms and grabbing his face. My paper towels fall down my dress to the floor, and I don't think anyone sees it except the cameraman, who is doing as instructed and catching everything. I double-cheek-kiss Terry, like I am still in Paris, I am so happy, and I don't smell a thing.

When everyone walks out, I pick up my wet paper towels and give the cameraman a wink.

"You did it!" he says smiling.

No, we did it, I think. Thousands of people contributed in some capacity, from money to prayers, well wishes to grace, and now we did it just as Ms. Harriett said we would.

"Can you drop me off at the Rosenbach Library?" I ask the cameraman. "And pass the pharmacy. I just need one thing."

That was the sweet smell of success.

Chapter 37

My phone rings. It's Dr. Hahn. I send her to voicemail.

"Hi Jeannine, it's Dr. Hahn from Penn Endocrinology reaching out to give you a few brief updates and check in on everything. Call me back at 555-5555. Thank you."

Breathe in Lorene Cary mumbling the Cramer's prayer of Thanksgiving, in *Ladysitting*: "And we most humbly beseech thee, O heavenly Father, so to assist us with thy grace, that we may . . . do all such good works as thou hast prepared for us to walk in."

Breathe out Dr. Hahn's brief updates and checking in on everything.

Chapter 38

Dear Ms. Harriett —

I am at the Rosenbach Museum & Library with you on my mind. Housed in a townhouse at 1865 Rittenhouse Square, this collection holds over 400,000 books including first edition Morrisons and first edition Hugheses and first edition Douglasses and first edition Wheatleys. This house was built during the time that you escaped to Philadelphia—so it's interesting to imagine you visiting the Rosenbach brothers. I am here to look through the partial archive of Lorene Cary's work that lives in the library's boxes and folders. It's hard to get an appointment to visit the Rosenbach's archives. And it's not often one gets to visit the archives of a living legend. The entire experience is insane. I know it is you who has brought us together again as I prepare to interview Lorene at the Collingswood Book Festival. She is as much a daughter to you as I am and therefore my big sister who feels more like an aunt than a friend. It's hard not to call her a genius. I already see a future in Philadelphia with her park, street sign, and statue. And coincidentally or divinely, this genius was opening her first play, *My General Tubman*, about you—Harriett Tubman, one mile from us at the Arden Theater while we were planning to open a bookshop in your name.

So, I wrote Lorene a letter:

Hello Ms. Cary:

I am Jeannine A. Cook. I recently attended your reading of *Ladysitting* at Drexel's Authors Cabaret where I received your email signed into the cover of a book.

I am writing because I am opening an independent bookshop in the Fishtown section of the city (258 E. Girard Ave.) with the mission of celebrating women writers, artists, and activists.

Now here's where this email gets interesting. The name of my new store is Harriett's Bookshop. It is named after Harriett Tubman (yes, I spell it with two t's), who I swear whispers in my ear from time to time. The opening for my bookshop is on Feb. 1, which coincidentally, and/or divinely, coincides with the run of your play, *Our General Tubman*, at the Arden Theater.

After carrying your books in my shop, attending your readings, and following your work with Safe Kids Stories, I had the idea to invite you here as the featured guest for my opening to christen my space, speak about your play, and share some wisdom with the community about our friend Harriett.

Please let me know if you can set aside 1-2 hours at any time on Feb. 1 for an event here at Harriett's. I will do everything in my power to make your visit worthwhile. If that means getting more copies of your book here, paying for your time, offering you my space for future events, I am willing to do almost anything to make this happen.

Okay, that's all for now. I am very excited to continue the conversation with you at your earliest convenience.

P.S. I've attached a few photos from Harriett's Bookshop.

Fingers crossed,
-j

Chapter 39

Dear Ms. Cook,

What a beautiful invitation. I've been trying to figure how I might make it work. Here's my problem: My daughter is coming from Vermont the night before, attending the matinee, and leaving that evening.

Right now, I'm at rehearsal, where I've been every day, since mid-December. So, when the rest of the family went up to visit her at the New Year, I stayed here with the production. I cannot miss her that one day.

Feb 2?

    Sent from phone, likely too fast

Chapter 40

"I'm not the kind of author people necessarily go out to see," Lorene told me as we waited for people to arrive at Harriett's for our first event.

"You're the kind of author I go out to see," I replied.

We had a mimosa bar and people chatted as the bookshop filled to standing room capacity. It was our first reading. My first time interviewing an author. She read a bit from her new memoir, *Ladysitting*, the story of caring for her one-hundred-year-old grandmother during the last year of her grandmother's life. Then she took audience questions. Lorene is captivating—no canned responses. Present. Smart. Thoughtful. Funny.

And just when we thought the event was over, I asked her about the myth versus the reality of Ms. Harriett and all of a sudden she turned the reading into a live performance, where Lorene was animated and walking around and grabbing things and enrolling the crowd while telling the story of the time you were on a ship on the waves of the Combahee River in 1863 using songs to call forth hundreds of enslaved people off of plantations toward a promised land.

Midway through the story, Lorene yanked the ice bucket off the mimosa bar that was filled with prosecco and orange juice and ice, and she told the bartender to remove the bottles. Then she hauled the ice bucket up onto her hair as she reenacted our ancestors running with everything they owned on their heads and their children on their backs. It was during this raid that Ms. Harriett became the first woman to lead a major military operation during the Civil War and earned the title General Tubman.

"Things could have gone very wrong if I dropped that ice bucket," Lorene whispered to me after the reading was over and all the books were signed and sold.

"Ice cold," I laughed, mocking Andre 3000. "Can I call you Tainty Lorene from now on?" I asked. "It's the Caribbean way of addressing your aunties—the women closest to your mother."

"Yes, I know. My people are from Barbados," she said, switching to a strong West Indian accent. "I can be your Tainty Lorene."

Chapter 41

Transcript excerpt from Lorene Cary's talk at Harriett's on February 2, 2020:

> Um, there is some, some Ashanti mythology and I say this, like, we say Christian mythology, it's some of the folk, folk stories about ancestors existing in the form of dolphin so that, and that's why the Cape May thing was [in my play].
>
> But your question was about mythologizing Harriett. Well, I think we create stories that we need, and sometimes it's conscious. People decided that they needed, we needed in Philadelphia for whatever reasons, we needed a female revolutionary hero, and they looked around and decided to make her that person. It's not that everybody was talking about Harriett's, it's that it was a decision that was made in Philadelphia partly because you needed a hero. We tell the story of Harriett Tubman running away, but the more nuanced stories we don't tell, the fact that her running away so affected people and the conversation among enslaved people, particularly in Chesapeake Bay, where there was lots of enslaved and free people like Philadelphia, like Pennsylvania slave and free, slave-free. So there was mixing and matching. There was so much

water travel in the Chesapeake Bay, and there were free people who were lumbering, doing water travel, we had lots of boats, every kind of little boat there was who could take somebody, put them in. Come on, come on, sit right here, you know, and then, and then they get out to someplace else, and then they're going to come back for you, like they had so many options in Maryland that something like 250 people left, sure like so Harriett personally took, you know, maybe 50 people or so, but other people would tell other people, do this. You don't do this. You can do that. She taught people.

Chapter 42

Dear Ms. Harriett,

I sit before a table at the Rosenbach Library with white gloves on, wondering where to begin as the archival librarian hands me folder after folder. Old drafts of Lorene Cary's unpublished poems, incomplete novels, folded drawings, meanderings, outlines. I even have one of the stories she wrote as a nine-year-old girl—"All we have is a partial collection," the librarian informed me. "This isn't even everything."

I want to see early drafts of her play, *My General Tubman*, but they don't have that.

Why are you guiding me back to Lorene again and again, Ms. Harriett? What am I looking for? What are you trying to tell me? What am I missing?

-j

Chapter 43

I think I am the last person boarding the plane back to Paris when who pops up behind me but Mrs. Graves. I don't look at her, try not to acknowledge her smug face, just continue looking forward to my seat. Maybe she's here with someone else, I think.

I find my row. Pull out my copy of *Ladysitting* and buckle up.

"It's gonna be a bumpy ride," Mrs. Graves whispers as she strolls past looking for her seat . . . "Extreme turbulence."

I'm just happy she's not trying to sit next to me. I try to get comfortable. Read *Ladysitting*.

"Remember me," Mrs. Graves doubles back, waving her hands closer and closer to my face. "I think you're in my place."

She squeezes into my row, puts her big butt in my face and sits on my lap.

"Please. Not today," I say as my calves cramp and Charlie horses race up and down my legs. Mrs. Graves is like a boa constrictor wrapping herself around each of my limbs. "Not now," I say as my thighs and toes tighten in knots.

"You keep testing me, huh?" Mrs. Graves says. "Why do you gotta walk so close to the edge? Rebelliousness is an Achilles heel."

I try not to respond but she hates to be ignored.

"Why you gotta be such a buzzkill?" I pull my copy of

Ladysitting from beneath her. "Why you gotta be so obsessive and controlling and manipulative and all in my space? It's my body."

The flight attendant walks by. "Excusez-moi," I say. My French is limited. I ask the flight attendant for water and search around in my bag for my medicine. My supply is getting low. I pop all three pills and gulp the water. *My body, my choice*, I tell myself. My leg muscles relax, but now it feels like a steel metal plate is lodged inside the left side of my head and slashing through my left eye. My left eye is blurry. I keep rubbing it because it burns and stings. I feel like bees are trying to claw their way out of my brain through the back of my left eye.

I should be celebrating a series of major accomplishments: I got the award, interviewed Nikole, got to Paris, started my novel, bought the building, finished the renovation, got the shop reopened, and visited the Lorene Cary archive, but I can't celebrate because Mrs. Graves is a queen bee using her stinger to inject venom into me. She is the queen bee of a hive that has been toyed with for too long. They all have jaws and claws. And they are all inside of me gnawing and stinging my body from the inside out until I wish I could jump from the plane.

"I wish you'd just leave me alone," I whisper as I try to close both eyes and embrace the awful sensation with affirmations of ease. Maybe I am just tired. It was a lot. Maybe I can reset my body if I fall asleep. The plane takes off and I am still awake. This is against my ritual and routine.

"You are stupid," I mumble under my breath. "Just leave me alone."

"You wanna rumble with the queen, huh?" Mrs. Graves raps Little Kim. "Throw a hex on your whole family. I'll show you how stupid ugly I can be, Mademoiselle Jeannine. I can show ya better than I can tell ya." Mrs. Graves and her swarm think I am a predator, and they attack me.

I spend the entire flight trying to fight back.

"Do it. Get it. I know you're thinking about it. What it will be like to just kill me and cut me out once and for all. But remember you'll be all alone after that. Lonely and slow moving. Uncreative and unmotivated. Remember I am your superpower, your secret weapon, the secret sauce. I fuel your fire. I've been with you since the beginning. Without me you are nothing. If you kill me, I won't ever come back. And you'll just be a dull lonely nobody nothing. You may as well kill yourself. Or pray Dr. Hahn can save you after you kill me."

I am shaking my head from side to side. My shadow self is like an autoimmune disease inflamed and fighting back with itself. Trying to get her and her hive out my body when I hear:

"Tout va bien, madame?" A French flight attendant hovers over me with a sad, desperate look in her eyes.

I just stare. I can't understand her or this.

"Want more water? Need something? A café? Some tea?" she switches to English.

I shake my head no uncontrollably. "I just need some . . . rest."

"Have some water," she insists. "You don't look so bien."

"Yeah, have some water," Mrs. Graves mocks. "That'll fix everything," she laughs.

"Do you have any la miel?" I ask the flight attendant. "Like cherie? Sweetness. Honey . . ."

"Honey?" She rushes off. "Yes, honey."

"This one?" she produces a packet right fast.

"Oui. Merci," I say in Philly French.

I just need to get back to Paris, back to Camille's asylum, back to writing. Back to sweetness.

"Wherever you are, there shall I be also," Mrs. Graves laughs. She gets up and walks away.

I go back to reading Lorene Cary's *Ladysitting*, which I've read three times now. It is the part where Nana gets stung by a bee on her hospital bed. Funny and awful. Visceral and amusing.

Just when it's getting to the good part, I hear:

"Mesdames et messieurs, bonjour. Le vol 999 en direction de Paris. Désolé pour les turbulences. La température extérieure est de 38 degrés, très chaud. N'oubliez pas de boire de l'eau."

Chapter 44

Dear Ms. Josephine,

I'm back. And "I'z married now." I feel like I went to Philly, gave birth, died and was resurrected. A lot can happen in just three days. But like I said, I'm back.

                                    C'est la vie.

                                            -j

Chapter 45

I crawl into my bed at Camille's asylum. And sleep and sleep and sleep. I tell Camille I am very tired. I have a fever. I am burning hot. A cough but no COVID. She insists something is going around. There are additional clinics built just for the Olympics. I walk to the closest French pharmacy. There is one on every other block. And they give me a paper with a list of local clinics, some open twenty-four hours. I Uber to the hospital and walk right in. I show my passport and within minutes I'm being examined. They do everything, a full-body workup. I tell the doctor my situation. I'm low on medicine and I need it. But I am also in Paris for the next six weeks. She prescribes me the medicine. I am in and out of the emergency room in less than an hour with a prescription that will be almost free at the local pharmacy. I take a Tylenol for my fever and I crawl back up into Camille's bed. Why can't it always be this easy?

After a few days, I wake up with enough strength to go to the BNF library and get back to writing. I have a pep in my step and a fierce urgency in my stride. I have characters who feel like friends that I want to hang out with, like Rose and Ray and Little Charlie and Big Charlie—the writer's group in the novel becomes my writer's group in real life. I like the fun of seeing the world through each of their eyes and writing prose and dialogue in each of their voices. I like that the narrator can get inside of their heads in close third person. Through Ray I get to be a stand-up comedian; through Rose I can write in flowery language about longing and beauty. Through Big Charlie and Little Charlie, I think about love triangles and entanglements with the living and the dead. The grandparents gave me a blueprint for a type of love that I hope will always exist. The sisters remind me of Walker's Nettie and Celie, Morrison's Nell and Sula, Singleton's Keke and Sza—a type of *Thelma and Louise*, sisterly friendship. I love all the dualities. I look forward to being with them more and more. Everywhere I go they come with me on the notes section in my phone. I add and take away from the novel, tweak and change their voices as I sit in a café eating French fries outside of the library at the foot of the Piscine Josephine. *This is the life I always wanted*, I think. It's the vision I saw for myself, but different. I really do get to be an author when I finish. And the thought made me write and write.

Chapter 46

"I know you're writing, Divine Nine," Camille says one morning when we run into each other at the corner café. "But there are some things you need for your journey ahead. I can't let you leave without them. Sit for a bit."

The French move at a slower pace. It slows my heart rate. But sometimes it throws me off balance. I want to get to the BNF early, but instead I agree to sit and have a café americano with extra sugars. "Yes, I know, so American," I say to the waiter.

"Have you been to the hammam?" Camille breaks in.

I have not.

She looks at me long and slow and silent. Takes a drag of her cigarette. "Hmmmm, okay. Well, that's where I think you need to go next. It's sacred and ceremonial, Divine Nine. You need to go get muddied and scrubbed." She blows out the left side of her mouth, licks her lips, and adds, "ASAP."

"Scrubbed?" I laugh, very confused.

"Soaked. Scrubbed. Steamed. But you definitely need to be scrubbed."

She tells me that when I go, I will have a menu of options. Just choose everything I can ever dream.

I guess this won't be a writing day.

Facial, wax, steam, sauna, exfoliation . . .

A few hours later I walk up to what looks like a Turkish café or a mosque or a dream, but there is a door to the left of the coffee drinkers marked "Hammam." Inside, various very large women point me from place to place until I reach a room with a menu and a woman on a pedestal who stands before me to take my order.

"This place is like a sanctuary," I tell the large woman standing on the pedestal.

"It is."

It has stained glass windows and stone walls. It's a colorful cave of sanctum and silence. No music plays. When I am done choosing, another large woman comes up to me and takes me to decide on a room for my shower. I have a hard time in public bathrooms and an even harder time in European public bathrooms. I get stuck in thoughts of human trafficking and germs, self-awareness and self-esteem. I have on very large white grandma panties, not realizing we are going to have to walk around half-naked wearing just our panties and bras. My panties are pulled high over my bulging belly and tighten slightly below my sagging breasts. I wish I had SKIMS. A matching set. Something practical that I wouldn't mind getting wet. A large woman points me toward the showers and gives me a large bar of black soap. Great. Black soap with white granny panties.

"Scrub," she says, handing me a series of different scrubbers: a hand one, a brush one, a puff. She points me toward the faucet. "Scrub. Rinse hot. Soak. Steam. Scrub. Rinse hot. Soak. Repeat."

After my third cycle, she grabs me by the shoulder and takes me to a table. "Hands on side."

I lie down on the stone table and do as I am told.

"Now we scrub."

I thought I had been scrubbing for the last hour but apparently had not.

She turns on the water and begins scrubbing me hard and soft, long and short, from my chest down to my toes. My eyes are closed. She feels like an octopus scrubbing every inch of me. It's kind of rough but kind of riveting like I am a baby. She washes my front and back several times. All I hear is running water, and a voice in my head saying Scrub. Rinse hot. Soak. Steam. Repeat. Until I am fading into a deep meditation or off to sleep. When she's done, she points me back to the shower. I feel like a layer of dirt has been released.

Camille meets me for lunch a few days later and asks me how it was.

"They can be a lil' rough, right?" She laughed. "But sometimes that's just what you need. Gotta shed that old skin."

"What's next?" I ask.

"I'll tell you in a few days," she laughs. "But for now you keep on writing. How many pages are you at?"

"About 20,000 words," I tell her.

"Okay, that tracks. Need me to read anything?"

I keep the pages close to my chest like Ms. Marie has told me and I don't share them with anyone. "Not yet."

Chapter 47

With just a few days left in Paris and about 23,982 words of the first draft of my novel complete, I get a request for an in-person interview at the Red Wheelbarrow by a young journalist who works remotely for a global organization based in Philly. We speak for three hours in a back area of the bookstore and Penelope, the owner, pops in several times during the interview to share her ideas, opinions, and conjecture.

Penelope and the Red Wheelbarrow are Paris staples in the 6th arrondissement, across from the Luxembourg Jardin. She has been instrumental in my pop-ups of Josephine's, and it is always good to spend time with other shopkeepers. When I think of the character of The Shopkeeper, as much as people think she's based on me, there's definitely quite a bit of Penelope in her character.

Although my business-self promised my writer-self this trip would have no business, the two sat down after a few arguments, compromised, and agreed this interview was okay.

(With permission to reprint)

JEANNINE A. COOK

Rooted in Legacy, Driven by Vision: Jeannine A. Cook's Journey from Philly to Paris, and Everything in Between
September 18, 2024
By: Jessica Barber

The ideas and plans began to take shape with mornings on the sacred land in Maryland where Harriett Tubman once helped her friends and family escape to freedom and afternoons spent in Tennessee where Ida B. Wells once taught children in Memphis using the power of her pen to denounce mob violence, poverty, and lynching to both national and international audiences. The time spent immersed in these environments, along with an impressive background of activism, writing, teaching, and an ever-growing passion for sharing knowledge and art and promoting accessibility to books, propelled Jeannine Cook to open Harriett's Bookshop in Fishtown, Ida's Bookshop in Collingswood, New Jersey, and enter the highly competitive literary scene to lay the foundations of a potential Josephine's Bookshop in Paris.

She didn't simply open the shops - she fought for years to be able to sign a check and call them her own. Each shop has the goal of creating a trustworthy and community-centered space and refuge that celebrates diverse voices and experiences, specifically that of women. Through reading stacks of literature about Wells and Tubman, speaking to historians, and visiting the places where they worked and lived, Cook was able to have an inner dialogue, a conversation if you will, to be able to shape her plans and create a vision for the shops.

Surmounting challenges that would lead most to throw their

hands up in the air and call it quits, she recently bought the building that Harriett's calls home, and has ambitions to keep it growing into an active community space, cafe, and wellness center. She slept on the floor of Harriett's during COVID, knocked on doors and sent out emails to donors, funders, and state offices, filled out grant applications, and conducted a series of interviews to make her vision come to life, all with limited luck. Over the course of a couple of years, people from all over the city, the country, and the world sent in small donations through an online fundraising campaign that empowered Jeannine to gain ownership of Harriett's.

In her writing and interviews, she often compares renting to sharecropping. The lack of ownership, both a historical and contemporary reality for many small businesses, **"translates into a limited ability to shape our destinies, make long-term investments, or build generational relationships."** Ultimately, it wasn't some big corporation, government grant, or private foundation that swept in to save the day and supply the funds – **it was the community**.

As I sat down with Jeannine to discuss all of this, the luxurious Luxembourg Gardens to our back, this foundational importance of community became a running theme of our conversation and a notable source of motivation for her to keep expanding and taking up space. We sat down around a worn wooden table stacked with scratches and piles of books to discuss her leap from Philadelphia to Paris over the past couple of years to pursue **an ambitious project of carving out a unique space where literature, community, and activism intersect, ultimately building upon what she has so thoughtfully constructed in the states.** Sitting together in the cozy Red Wheelbarrow Bookstore, one of the handful of anglophone bookshops scattered across the French capital, we discussed the challenges, successes, plans, and hopes that have arisen in her ambitious decision to go global.

Jeannine first came to the cultural capital on a scholarship to study James Baldwin when her inner dialogue and conversation with Josephine began. She was clear from the start - she was not there by accident or to follow narrowly personal ambitions. Just as she has listened to and been guided by Harriett and Ida, she spoke extensively about her need to step into the world of Josephine Baker, another extraordinary **heroine, activist, visionary and complex Black woman who once danced, spied, sang, advocated, and walked the streets of Paris**.

After having left the United States during the era of strict Jim Crow Laws and extreme racial violence, Baker headed to Europe, like many other Black Americans during the 20th century (Baldwin, Charlie Parker, Eugene Jacques Bullard, W.E.B. Du Bois, and Langston Hughes, to name a few). Her achievements in her adopted country became so numerous and applauded that she went on to become the first and only Black woman to be awarded the Legion of Honor, one of France's highest honors, and inducted in the Panthéon mausoleum.

In a symposium hosted at the American University of Paris in 2023, where Josephine's daughter Marianne was present, Jeannine channeled Josephine's bygone era with a new sense of energy fit to challenge the problems society is facing today. Books about Baker's life and other novels and works of nonfiction detailing Black Americans' life in Paris, as well as major classic works of literature that primarily seek to center female authors, were loaded into Jeannine's carry-on luggage after problems with shipment and delays. The show needed to go on, and Jeannine hadn't crossed the Atlantic for nothing.

The symposium, as well as a temporary installation of what will hopefully one day be a permanent Josephine's Bookshop in Paris, served as a cultural safe space for many Black American expats living in Paris, Jeannine told me. While the installation and symposium constituted a major success, the challenges that lie ahead are many. In the very room we were sitting in to have our interview was located on one of the most precious real-estate strips in Paris, a series of art galleries, high-end French bistros, antique shops, and designer stores where many of the owners inherited the property from family trees that span centuries. We were just a short walk from the Panthéon as well, where Baker was inducted in 2021. Many of the more recent businesses are not able to buy the building they're located in, which would cost millions, but instead opt to purchase a lease at a price point still much higher than the French, or American, national average. The problem of real estate in such a highly sought after city coupled with the exorbitant price of importing English books post-Brexit creates a maze of problems. Add the laborious labyrinth of French bureaucracy into the equation and the whole endeavor feels like an endless uphill battle.

But I was speaking to a woman who had faced one challenge after another and refused to succumb to complacency. She has sold books on horseback and on the street corners of universities, works with youth who are often in very precarious situations, and successfully bought a building with a price tag over $700k. As I said, she isn't one to throw her hands in the air in defeat.

To this effect, she told me, "It's like a flower - I can't just make it open because I want it to. But I know it will bloom eventually, then I can sit back and say, 'damn that's beautiful, I'm so glad I've just let it be.' I believe that Josephine's will happen in her own time and way." She recently made an offer to the owner of Ida's Medicis at 9 rue de Medicis and eagerly awaits a response on purchasing his lease.

At the end of the day, it's not about personal achievement or even the potential glamor and prestige that comes with owning a Parisian storefront. It comes back to serving the same community that got her to where she is today, even if it means facing immense economic challenges. **It's about building a global overground underground railroad**. We discussed at length the exponential growth of enormous corporations and multi-million dollar enterprises that swallow local businesses in a system that often centers the "I" instead of the "we." France doesn't have large bookstore chains like Barnes and Noble, and Amazon, while growing in popularity, has still not reached the same market size as the U.S.

When I asked her what types of lessons she has learned since "going global," she told me, "I believe that the experiences I'm having are happening so that I can understand the problems, point them out, and facilitate solutions. The global economy, from the perspective of small businesses, has a lot of work to do. No one bats an eye that McDonalds is here, but when people see a small bookshop attempt to take up space, people ask how is that possible because it's incredibly difficult. And it shouldn't be."

These problems, while they may be heightened between certain sets of borders, are not unique to one country or another - **they reflect a global phenomenon**. Jeannine has been able to stay motivated by frequently invoking the spirit of Ida B. Wells, as well as Baker and Tubman, in her advocacy and projects, drawing parallels between historical struggles against oppression and current challenges faced by independent bookstores and threats to intellectual freedom.

The community that she has slowly and scrupulously begun to form has been able to lift up her efforts as well. All of the networking opportunities and contacts she had made in Paris, whether it be with her partners at American University, with authors like Sylvia Serbin, Terri Simone, Ajiri Aki, and Jake Lamar, with other expats (many of which come from Philly), notably Lindsey Tramuta, Denise King, Camille Rich, and Maria Bello or with the owner of Red Wheelbarrow, Penelope Fletcher, is a reflection of the collective community care that often springs up in the book world, a mindset that is progressively disappearing in the contemporary capitalist landscape of our age.

To this, she added, "Coming from and being raised in Black southern culture, we just learn how to take care of each other by moving in the same ways that Harriett would have on the underground railroad or Josephine did as a spy. You're taking care of your people without it being for commercial gain. A lot of it happens in silence."

Even after presenting her case to several officials, armed with fact sheets and examples of French law that promotes literacy and protects bookstores and libraries, no large scaled funding has trickled in just yet. Through Jeannine's lens, building a community and networking in Paris has reflected **this need to take care of one another in order to succeed**, because there is no one stepping in and assuming the responsibility, nor is there robust infrastructure in place to support small businesses on a global scale.

And again, despite these setbacks, the plans for expansion continue. Crossing over to another continent, Jeannine has also begun to have the similar conversation she's had with Tubman, Wells, and Baker with Wangarĩ Maathai, a Kenyan political activist, feminist, and environmentalist of the 20th century who led the successful Green Belt Movement that planted over a million trees in the country after British colonialism and empowered thousands of women to stand up for their rights. In honor of **the first African woman to win the Nobel Peace Prize**, Jeannine has been in close contact with the still-active movement in preparation of the 20th anniversary of Maathai receiving the prize. Plans to weave a bookshop into the planned year-long dedication are in the works with a producing partner, Cthrough Productions, on the ground - a refreshing fact given the struggles she's had bringing English books to Paris.

With this on the horizon, the plans in Paris are continuing to form and evolve in parallel. Jeannine wants to design the next Josephine's Bookshop installation as a reconstruction of Baker's childhood tenement home in Saint Louis. She spent the summer working on a novel and a memoir thanks to her renowned agent, Marie Brown, who helped her land a two book deal with Amistad/HarperCollins. And she also recently launched a campaign to send ten Philly youth to Paris after a twelve week credit bearing course. Most of the students have no passports, have never been on a plane, and formerly dropped out of traditional high schools. She is hopeful that with community support, they will head to Paris to study Baldwin and Baker this November.

Often overshadowed by her work as a war hero, spy, and performer, Josephine Baker was also a passionate advocate and activist for youth. She adopted twelve children from all over the world to form what she called her **"rainbow tribe"** with the goal of showing that "united children from different races, raised together as siblings, have no animosity; that racial hate is not natural. It's an invention by mankind." **Jeannine wants to channel that sense of inclusiveness and expanded opportunity to allow young Philadelphians to go global as well.**

At the root of this mission, she wants to combat low literacy rates and deteriorating reading levels, for both youth and adults. "The entire book industry—stores, agents, authors, publishers, etc. get to see increasing literacy levels as our collective cause. If we don't, **we are complicit in our own demise.**" She is working to bring students to Paris, but also has plans to construct libraries at existing youth program spaces, such as Aaron Campbell's "Level Up" in West Philadelphia and Building African American Minds in Easton, Maryland, as well as continuing to employ young adults in her bookshops.

She asks the question, "what happens in a place where people are not literate and are not able to fully communicate their thoughts and ideas through words?" More often than not, it creates an environment where violence proliferates and communities are torn apart. That is what she is fighting against with these community partnerships, plans to go abroad, and the ongoing initiatives of Ida's and Harriett's.

I began to wrap up the conversation with a question that kept resurfacing in my mind: "After the challenges you encountered in finally securing your own space in Philadelphia and understanding how significant ownership was for you personally and for the community, you now find yourself in Paris. After what may have felt like an uphill journey, you're still expanding, still growing, and still seeking to inspire. I have to ask—**what drives you to stay motivated and keep all these projects going?**"

She burst into a laugh that resounded off the book-covered walls. "I'm a time traveler. I spend time in the past, in the present, and the future and I often feel like it all starts to blend together. I try to think about what it might be like for my great-great-great-grandchildren and envision a future for them. I really wish that I could have that knowledge from my ancestors, but because so many of them were illiterate, including my great-grandmother. I don't have anything in that way – I have to pull it up out of my own genetics or read other people's stories. I think about what I'm leaving for somebody else, what kind of legacy and tools I can give them so they can keep going, and that gives me fuel."

In closing, she emphasizes that bringing these exciting projects to life requires not only the belief of the community but also the support and investment of government, corporations, businesses, and organizations with the financial resources to make the vision a reality and make Philadelphia a viable part of the global conversation.

"I can envision a different possibility and reality as a time traveler, just like Baker, Tubman, and Wells once did. I just want to say, you know, come on because you're slowing down the progress."

As the "queen of the curveball," Jeannine A. Cook consistently turns obstacles into stepping stones, driving her bold vision of community, activism, and global literary spaces forward with unwavering resilience. **Philadelphia, and the world, need more bold visionaries like her.**

Chapter 48

After the interview I buy a copy of the book *Until August* by Gabriel García Márquez from Penelope because the title seems fitting. I ask her to take my photo in front of 9 rue de Medicis, a former bookstore space I dream of as a permanent location for Josephine's. She tells me she's always wanted to write a novel, but running her bookstore takes everything she's got. I tell her there's no time like the present and challenge her to start. We agree that we'd make great neighbors. I hug Penelope and leave to read the entire book down the street sitting down at Treize Bakery eating Southern-inspired French cuisine.

Until August was published by Márquez's sons posthumously on what would have been his ninety-sixth birthday. The story is about a woman whose mother has passed away. To grieve every year, despite her happy marriage, she escapes for the month of August to the island where her mother is buried to take flowers and sleep with a random man in hopes that the ritual will keep her sane and close to her mother in some way. It was written during the days of Márquez's declining mental and physical health, which shows in the writing. It includes his handwritten notes, disorientation, and confusion. I love it and hate it. The whole idea of the book makes me angry and happy, devastated and sad—but mostly motivated to write before the day comes when I cannot.

I go to the BNF and write and write and write.

Chapter 49

I wake to a call from Mama Sonia Sanchez. It's 2:22 a.m. Paris time. "My dear sister, did I wake you?" she speaks in sweet poetry.

I sit up and get myself together. "Is everything okay?" I don't want to lie and I don't want to tell the truth, so I ask a question.

"I am fine, it's . . . you crossed my mind," she says.

It gives me a warm feeling that I could cross someone's mind.

"I am in Paris, again," I tell her.

"Oh, that's right, yes . . . you have a bookshop there . . . now . . . right?"

"Kind of. Yes. This time I am here to write," I say.

"I want the tee shirt," she says. She tells me she has all my other tee shirts from my other campaigns. "You remind me of the time I wrote a play there."

I didn't know about her play.

"And they translated it into French."

Didn't know about that either.

"I am a poet and a playwright. It's okay to be a lot of things. Well, I won't hold you, my dear sister, just calling to tell you to keep going. Don't get distracted."

I wonder where she's really from and how she always knows just what to say.

I thank her for calling and promise to put her tee shirt in the mail even though I don't have any Josephine's Bookshop tee shirts, but if Mama Sonia Sanchez asks you for a tee shirt at 2 a.m. on a Tuesday, you find a way.

Chapter 50

Dear Ms. Josephine—

Today is my last day in Paris. It's so cloudy. I think it will rain. I am so sad, I could vomit. Lovesick.

I know I have things to do and people to see in Philly. But it turns my stomach in knots to go back home with this book unfinished—what if it never gets done like Márquez's *Until August*. You know how many writers I know who want to finish a book, yet never do?

I return to Philly with more on my plate than before I left. The Indie Bookstore Crawl, a Back-to-School sale, author visits, the youth conductors, board meetings, an incomplete café, donations, payroll, book orders, book debt, book requests, etc. And I love every second of it. It's so Harriett's. It's just not so Josephine's.

It doesn't mean I don't want to go back, I just wonder if my writer self needs Paris and my business self needs Philly, then what's a girl to do? Overthinking is my character flaw. Every protagonist has one. It's what fuels the hero's journey. Eventually I am gonna have to face the climax. Have both, neither, choose, or be forever pulled in two. Shit or get off the pot as my friend's nana used to say. At least I go back to Philly with 31,324 more words outside of me. Better out than in. I can see the light at the end of the tunnel, Ms. Josephine.

    Thanks for being such a great listener!

-jeannine

Chapter 51

On my last day in Paris, Camille tells me she wants to take me out for a drink.

This is the first time on my journey that I want to tell her no thanks. She can see it in my face.

"Not that kind of drink, silly," she says. "There's water . . . it comes out of the ground."

I still want to say no. Drinking dirty water off the ground is actually where I draw my esoteric line. But she asks me to trust her. Everything is unfolding in perfect order.

We walk to the top of a hill. "This is an artesian well." Camille points at a big silver apparatus as I catch my breath. "It's a natural fountain of holy water that explodes up from the ground on its own," she explains. Discovered by monks in the Middle Ages, these wells carry their own source of energy and warmth. "I know what you're thinking, but this water is clean, Nine. It's been tested many times and somehow this water remains pure."

"It's a miracle," I say to Camille using my app to translate the inscription plaque that explains the history of the well. At certain spots in the world, water defies gravity.

Elders and children, teenagers and parents line up behind Camille and me in silence with jugs to collect their supply of holy water. "People use it for everything, Nine. They come from all over to find this water. It heals and protects."

Camille hands me a jar. "Fill it," she says as others drink the water profusely from cups and mugs and cupped hands.

I use my jar to collect the crystal-clear water that volcanoes out. These wells were drilled by Carthusian monks in the 1100s. It was at these miracle spots that early churches and monasteries were built for a simple reason: flowing water meant life could be sustained and communities could be built. Carthusian monks use holy water to this day to help purify their souls.

"My cup runneth over," I joke as holy water overflows from my jar. "For real." I put a top on my jar. And hand my other jar to Camille to fill up her cup.

It makes me think of a story from my childhood when my dad once called me into the bathroom. I was about eight.

"Yesssss, Daddy," I said, thinking I was in trouble.

"You believe in miracles?" he said.

"Yes," I said, knowing about miracles from Sunday school—an extraordinary event that brings great consequences.

"You ever seen one?" His eyes bulged.

I stood puzzled.

"A miracle. Have you ever seen one?"

"No . . ." I said.

"Okay, well today I am going to show you a miracle. I am going to show you how to walk on water, so you can teach your children's children's children's children."

No, I didn't think my dad with his skinny ankles and ashy feet and crusted toenails was going to walk on water. No, I did not believe him at first. But also knowing him, I thought maybe he might.

"Now watch." He began filling the tub with hot water. "You still don't believe me, do you? That I know how to walk on water?"

I did not.

He sat on the side of the tub with his hands in praying position as the water rose higher and higher in the tub.

Hands clasped together and his bulging eyes now shut, he started: "Lord, if it be thy will, let me show my daughter one of your many miracles. Let me show her how to walk on water. Please, Lord. Please," he pleaded. "Only if it be thy will. So that she will believe."

And then my father stood up, walked over to the tub, turned off the water, which was close to overflowing, and held his hands up to the sky. He cried out once more, "If it be thy will."

He put his big toe on the water. "Hot." He snatched his foot back and laughed. Then he tested the water with his hands and flicked it off in my face, and a few drips got on my shirt and a few drips hit the ground. "That is a blessing for you," my dad said as I wiped the water from my face. He paced back and forth in front of me one time, two times, three times, silently pleading with the heavens to help him show me a miracle. And on the third time he shouted, as he hovered his foot over the bath water again, "Thank you, Lord."

He pulled his foot back and started his happy dance.

"You did not walk on water," I interrupted his praise.

"You missed it?" he said. "The miracle?"

"I think I missed it," I said.

"I'll do it again, then. But you have to pay close attention."

Again, he went over to the filled bathtub. Put his big toe in and then snatched it back out. "Hot." Again, he bent over the tub to take a splash of water in his hand once more. He sprinkled it in my face, and it bounced off onto the carpet in front of us. Then he walked back and forth over the carpet like he was waiting for something to happen.

He broke out in a spirit of praise that his body couldn't handle. His arms flailing. I still didn't see anything happen.

"See that water?" He pointed to a few droplets on the ground. "I'm walking on it."

"You can, too," he laughed and let me take a turn. "Walk on the water," he insisted. Then we both danced around that bathroom barefoot like we'd discovered something profound.

There was a Clark Sisters song in my children's choir that we had to memorize and sing month after month at the top of our little lungs,

> "Looking for a miracle
> Expect the impossible."

"What is a miracle?" I asked the choir director.

"An extraordinary event that brings VERY welcome consequences," she had replied.

"Take a sip," Camille says, bringing me back to the present.

I open my jar and drink from it with full expectation that it will taste like dirt, but it does not.

"It's a miracle." I smile at Camille. "Better than Dasani!"

We laugh.

"I appreciate you, Nine," she tells me while searching in her bag for a lighter. "I don't know what's next for you on this journey, my friend, but I trust that whatever you've gotten here at La Porte Bleue helps you get to the end of this story."

I thank Camille by touching my hand to the ground at the base of her feet.

"Yes, it will."

And I'm off.

Chapter 52

Liturgy of Literacy

Holy mothers

Full of grace

Blessed be Saint Maya of Stamps, daughter of Bailey

Blessed be Saint Phillis of Banjul daughter of sables

Blessed be Saint Lorraine of Nanny daughter of The Gourd

Grant us your presence

Now and in the hour of our deaths.

How much have we learned from our predecessors, the keepers of thine word, of their accounts of the ancients and have found it written in their acts. This day let it be anointed by the great appointed and accepted tribunal gathering of elders, that endowed within their wisdom is the right to declare, debate, and decree on the veneration of our lettered saints.

Holy mothers

Full of Grace

Blessed be Saint Zora of Notsulga, who watches God

Blessed be Saint Bell of Berea, who devoted to love bore the fruit of Veodis

Blessed be Saint Toni of Lorain, who held words holy and characters charitably, made worthy, when on earth, to possess a miraculous pen. Encouraged by this thought, we implore you to obtain for us

Now and in the hour of our death—sacred land, sacred space, sacred communion.

Certain of you, desirous of participating in so holy a work, be implored to decide with whom you walk and with whom you invoke. We give heed to your devotion, and beseech thee to prepare a presentation of the names of the martyrs and the miraculous of whom you want the tribunal to debate and decree.

Holy mothers

Full of grace

Blessed be Saint June, of architecture, solid gospel sanctified;

Blessed be Saint Margaret of Birmingham, daughter of famine and jubilee;

Blessed be Saint Faith of Tar, daughter of textiles and Posey

Grant us your presence

Now and in the hour of our deaths.

Now I lay me down to sleep,

I pray the Lorde my Soul to keep[;]

If I should die before I 'wake,

I pray the Lorde my Soul to take

We grant you by these present documents, with our full Universal Authority, free permission to circulate petition and submit confirmation to members of this divine order for concretization.

Holy mothers

Full of grace

Blessed be Saint Lucille, of Depew the elegist;

Blessed be Saint Gwendolyn the chronicler daughter of Keziah, and shikaakwa;

Blessed be Octavia of Spiritus; daughter of trilogy and Pasadena

Grant us your presence

Now and in the hour of our deaths.

Take this as your buckler of protection as ye go forth.

Amen

Ase

SECTION III:
SEPTEMBER 2024

Jeannine A. Cook interviews Nikki Giovanni

JEANNINE A. COOK: How? How do we do this?

NIKKI GIOVANNI: We have always took the least and made it the best.

Chapter 53

When I get back to Philly, and then back to Harriett's, it is time to go back to school.

For about a year I've been working with a collective of local educators, activists, artists, behavior health professionals, travel agents, students, parents, media partners, and neighbors designing a project I introduced called "Philly in Paris."

After several of my own trips back and forth to Paris, I feel strongly that the next installation of Josephine's Bookshop should be dedicated to those deemed to be at-risk youth. I ask myself—how much would it change a life to have an opportunity to go from Philly to Paris? It radically changed my life, but is it enough to change others? It's a gift I want to give, though I barely have it for myself. I call it literary exposure therapy. The idea that one can overcome personal trauma simply by experiencing new stories, new people, new places, and new intentional plot twists—new jawns.

I pull together a team and do what I do best, create space. I realize I am still just designing curriculum like back in my American Friends Service Committee days. "To whom much is given, much is required," I tell myself. "Everything is unfolding in perfect order," I tell myself. But also, "Why the hell am I doing this to myself?"

Sometimes community building works and sometimes it

does not. I tell people collaboration is the hardest soft skill to adopt. Community building is a practice that takes many iterations and adaptations. You're not gonna get it right on the first shot. It's supposed to be messy. It's supposed to be fragile, it's supposed to shift and crack and break apart, but over time things settle and faux community is replaced with real community and leaders emerge. Books and stories give us a common language for grounding. They ground us and anchor us and provide a place of solace in the face of howling wind. The bookshop serves as a backdrop, a meeting house, a sacred space, and what I call creative organizing through protest art takes place. The Philadelphia Citizen calls my work literary activism. I just call it a lot.

I take a book and not only invite a community to read it together, but to become it, to embody the story and fully try it on. I hope that in the unpacking we dive deeper into trust and world building, and new relationships emerge. Not just mere conversation, but deeper respect for one another. I've moved from the performative to the ceremonial, the absurd to the surreal. From factories, to theaters, from books as picket signs, to postcards as protection, from petitions to social posts, from horse barns to backyards, and now there's Philly in Paris.

Philly in Paris is my most recent protest—an act of creative rebellion against the redundancy of systems who host block parties and banquets instead of seeking out innovative and bold measurable solutions. I want to re-engage out-of-school youth and design a model for interrupting cycles of violence, bringing different sectors together to complete a full cycle of one measurable act of change. It's why we've had youth conductors working in the bookshop since the beginning, so when I retire they can continue this thing.

Whenever I invite people together in a group, anywhere in the world, that community never has to commit to working together forever. All we need to do is complete the next thing in front of our faces. Do one simple act.

This cohort commits to taking ten YESPhilly youth from the School District of Philadelphia's Opportunity Network from Philly to Paris. The youth don't have passports and none of them have ever been on an airplane. We commit to making this a credit-bearing course for the School District of Philadelphia so there's a replicable model in place.

I commit to raising the funds independently in sixty to ninety days.

It's like walking on water, I tell myself with a laugh and a sigh and a whimper, and for weeks I don't write a thing. I am up early and late trying to figure out how to make the numbers fit together in this broken block chain.

It's important to me that we work with youth from YESPhilly—an alternative school for youth who have dropped out of traditional schools. It is my only strong request. I have worked intermittently from 2007 to 2019 for YESPhilly in some capacity or another and this feels to me like an extension of that ongoing work. It's like the part of my mission that I can't seem to figure out. I even wrote my master's thesis in 2014 about how to re-engage out-of-school youth, interviewing everyone from program directors to parents. One of my solutions has always been world building—exposure to new worlds makes you deeper.

The goal was to raise $60,000 to take ten youth and four chaperones from Philly to Paris by November for a seven-day stretch that also happens to fall during Thanksgiving and my birthday. This was a project I started before I knew my debut novel would also be due in October, so now I have to figure out how to clone myself or split myself in two.

We have only three months to raise the money and get the youth there over the holiday break. I have three months to find the climax of my novel—which I can't seem to figure out how to approach for days. I want someone to teach the youth about Josephine and Baldwin and international travel and global economics and all the things.

Only now I am on another deadline with sweet but firm emails from my editor checking in, like, "Hey Jeannine?"

And yes, keep the bookshop afloat with meetings from Keke Palmer's team for an event in the spring and another so-called celebrity author who will remain nameless—I finally refuse to host her because her team asks if I can host her book event but not speak at my own bookshop. That's insane.

And finally, a highlight of my season, we have Alexis Pauline Gumbs coming into town at the end of the month to speak about Audre Lorde for a book event in my friends' backyard that we are calling "Homegirls & Handgrenades"—for these events I invite a surprise interviewer to discuss the book with the author. It's fun and cinematic and it feels like a game show to me. I love that it feels like a game.

On the side, I push toward adding the café into Harriett's, which requires all new plumbing and new HVAC and a cappuccino machine, a grinder, and a laundry list of other things.

Oh, and another fun project, look cute for interviews, 'cause I want my great-great-grandchildren to look back at pictures and like my outfits. I get a call from Sarah Lomax and Tayyib Smith to interview Sonia Sanchez at the Philadelphia Museum of Art's next book-related celebration. My workload is insane. And yes, some days I love it and some days I love it and complain.

Scrub. Rinse. Rest. Repeat. I laugh and cry and scream.

I ask my good sister friend of twenty years, Blaire, to lead the Philly in Paris collective because I know I have to write, and I know Blaire never gives up. We went to the University of the Arts together and then ended up as neighbors living Down the Bottom. She commits to being in the classroom with the youth for one hour for two to three days a week for the next twelve weeks as we prepare for takeoff.

Chapter 54

But the other reason I ask Blaire to lead the Philly in Paris collective is her seventeen-year-old son, who I call my nephew. He is officially home from juvenile placement (again!) but still on probation. I've gone to court and written letters, and the judge agrees that Nephew can come out, work in the bookshops, and attend the Paris trip if he stays away from his gang. I feel like the Philly in Paris project could save us all. I make writing a part of Nephew's job at Harriett's. He completes this essay and gets it published in a local publication, *Generosity*.

Dreaming Beyond the Block
Category: Op-ed
Nephew

I am a 17 year old Black male from Down The Bottom in West Philadelphia. I've become too familiar with the sound of sirens and the cold feel of handcuffs. Gun charges became part of my life early on, not because I was out to cause trouble, but because it felt like I had no other choice. When it doesn't feel safe out, you have to protect yourself. Who else will protect you? "Rather be caught with it than die without it", became the mindset for me and my friends. I'm only 17, but my encounters with the law started way before I even hit my teenage years. The first time I was arrested, I was 12 years old. My friends and I were walking around downtown, checking if car doors were unlocked. It wasn't anything serious to us at the time, just looking for loose change or chargers, but it landed me in a holding cell, staring at my mother's disappointed face.

The moment that changed everything for me was when the attorney general's office kicked in our door. My mom was sick, throwing up into a trash can while agents searched our house. My siblings were still in their pajamas, terrified, and my little sister, who was only five, cried, wrapped in a blanket while being carried down the stairs. Seeing my mom, sick and begging them to let her comfort my sister, made me realize that this wasn't the life I wanted for my family or my community.

I've watched friends fall into the same cycle of incarceration (or death), their potential snuffed out before they even had a chance to make something of themselves. For us, carrying guns wasn't about being tough — it was survival. But sitting in placements and the Youth Study Center made me realize that change was necessary, not just for me, but for all the young men stuck in this same situation.

During my time in placement, I became known as "the lawyer" because I would help other kids understand their charges and file grievances. So many of them didn't even know their basic rights. The staff treated us like we weren't worth anything, denying us basic human rights. I saw kids get hurt in ways that still stick with me, like at my graduation when one of the guys handed out pamphlets with his eye bloodshot and damaged after being restrained by staff. That's not how we should be living.

That's why the collective my mom and aunt started, Philly in Paris, is so important. We want to break this cycle of despair and create opportunities for young Black men and women like me to see that there's more to life than just surviving Philly's streets. We've raised almost $20,000 but need another $40,000 to make this happen by November. This program includes a 10-week course to prepare us for the trip, but more than that, it's about closing the exposure gap that holds so many of us back.

Less than 6% of students who study abroad are students of color, and that number hasn't changed in over two decades. But for those who do, there's an 18% increase in graduation rates. We've seen firsthand what these experiences can do for young people. For us, it's not just a trip—it's a chance to see that the world is bigger than West Philly, bigger than the violence, the guns, and the fear.

I am at work now, trying to stay focused on a better future. But when I think about stepping off a plane in Paris, it feels like stepping into another life. Imagine a young guy from Philly, usually walking around with a hoodie and a ski mask, always watching his back. Now picture him walking through the streets of Paris, where he doesn't have to worry about who's watching. He can breathe, relax, and just be normal for once. That's what Philly in Paris is about — showing us that there's more out there, that we can dream beyond the block.

For me, Paris is more than just a trip. It's a chance to rediscover myself. I used to be artistic as a kid, good with colors and designs, but somewhere along the way, I forgot that. I had to focus on surviving. Going to Paris could remind me, and other young men like me, that there's more to life than just getting by. We could see that success doesn't always come through money or power, but through creativity, passion, and the connections we make.

In a way, Philly in Paris is like a conductor — leading the way, just like Harriett Tubman did, but instead of escaping enslavement, we're showing young people a path out of the "slavery" of the jail system. This program is about creating a way out of the life that traps so many of us.

Chapter 55

The next week Nephew goes to jail (again!).

Chapter 56

I allow my body to sink into a sea of deep despair for the Nephews of the world. I let the tide take me under and I say things like "I can't" because I can't read or write or think. And "I give up" on the Nephews because they make my heart ache. Lorene's prose don't help. Ms. Harriett can't help. Ms. Sonia can't help. And neither does Ms. Josephine. Even Mrs. Graves stays away. All I do is sleep on my pink paisley couch and hum:

> Oh my Lorde, Lorde, Lorde, Lorde,
> Mmmm, hmmm
> Oh my Lorde, Lorde, Lorde, Lorde,
> Mmmm, hmmm
> Oh my Lorde, Lorde, Lorde, Lorde,
> Mmmm, hmmm
> Oh my Lorde, Lorde, Lorde, Lorde,
> Mmmm, hmmm
> Audre of Gertrude
> Mmmm, hmmm
> Of Carriacou
> Mmmm, hmmm
> Symmetric named
> Mmmm, hmmm
> Nearsighted and blind

Mmmm, hmmm
Tongue tied truth teller
Mmmm, hmmm
God of Goddesses
Mmmm, hmmm
A Biomythologist
Mmmm, hmmm
Erotic powertress
Mmmm, hmmm
Story books on a table
Mmmm, hmmm
Sister outsider a song
Mmmm, hmmm
Angel seeing bursts of light
Mmmm, hmmm
Scratching the surface of life
Oh my Lorde, Lorde, Lorde, Lorde,
Mmmm, hmmm
Oh my Lorde, Lorde, Lorde, Lorde,
Mmmm, hmmm
Oh my Lorde, Lorde, Lorde, Lorde,
Mmmm, hmmm
Oh my Lorde, Lorde, Lorde, Lorde

Chapter 57

"What about the others?" my dad texts randomly. "What about your book?"

I look at my phone and put it on Do Not Disturb.

Chapter 58

Dear Ms. Harriett—

You said wade in the water, and now I'm drowning.

-jeannine

Chapter 59

Harvey comes over again and again. And one day, I finally let him in.

"You should go away . . ." he says as he enters my near-empty apartment.

"No, *you* should go away," I snap, lying back down.

"And write," he says.

No response.

"And take a shower," he says.

No response.

"And eat something."

I am not hungry. I like my smell. I cannot write.

No response.

"I can get you a ticket to Canada," he says.

"Canada? What am I supposed to do in Canada?"

"Escape. Run away. Leave. Never come back."

"I don't want to run away to Canada. It's too cold."

"Where do you want to go, then, Jeannine? You can't just sit on the couch for the rest of your—"

"I wanna go home," I blurt out. "I want to go back to Virginia and sit by the water. I want to go home."

"Well, then to your grandmother's house you go."

Chapter 60

"Nana."

She says, "Yes," from the other side of the phone. I am scared to ask her if I can come stay in her back room in Newport News, Virginia, for a few days. She has lived alone since my grandfather passed away two years ago and the house is not the same. I think she's enjoying the time by herself (or at least she never complains) and I can imagine it feels pretty good not having to take care of others the way she has most of her life, even though that's not something I think she'd ever say.

"Jeannine?" My nana is a gregarious, sassy Southerner with big hips, wide hugs, and Northerner instincts. Born in the South, she moved to Brooklyn during the Great Migration, then raised my father (and many others) for decades before returning down south to Newport News.

She jokes and laughs even more than my dad.

When I was a kid, Nana would ask, "You want me to spank him?" when my dad left the room.

And I'd nod my head yes. "He needs a spanking."

"What did he do this time?" she'd whisper. They'd both be making fun, holding back laughter, him hiding around the corner waiting for my response, but I was always serious.

"He just don't listen," I'd say.

"Okay, I'm gonna spank him," she'd respond and then they'd both crack up.

All three of us are Sagittarius—the ninth zodiac sign spanning November 22 to December 21. Sagittarius are characterized as adventurous and free-spirited with a blunt approach to saying what they want to say. Nana is straight as an arrow with her words. "Say what you trying to say, granddaughter," she says.

"Can I come stay with you for a few days?" I whisper like someone might hear and find out I'm not okay.

She's quiet for longer than I'd prefer. So I try to think of how to politely respond if she says no.

"Of course," she says.

"And write." I continue to overexplain. "I need a place to write the end of my book."

"I already said yes, chile, just tell me what days."

"You don't have to cook no big meal or anything."

"I know—"

"But what about your salmon with squash? Or your turkey wings?"

"We'll see how I'm feeling," she laughs. "Might be canned tuna and wing dings."

I laugh for the first time in weeks.

"Nana, can you keep it a secret that I'm coming? I just want to stay in your back room and write—no interruptions, no expectations, no interjections, no favors, no requests, no costume changes, no timeline, just me and my story. I have the final act of this book to complete and just need a few days to hear what myself is trying to say to me."

"So don't tell your father you're coming, is what you're saying?"

"Don't tell anyone, not even Daddy's leg, Lester, that I'm coming. I need to focus."

Nana is a vault. If you ask her to hold something, she will lock it up and throw the key in the ocean.

In my forty years of life, I've never overheard her tell anyone's business. She doesn't take her job as matriarch lightly.

"It's kind of perfect 'cause I have a doctor's appointment, too; if you come take me it'll save someone else the trip."

"Absolutely," I say.

I've never stayed alone with her—just Nana and I. It feels like I am living inside of Lorene's *Ladysitting* book about her nana, because I keep reading it over and over again and now I am here with my nana too—only she is ladysitting me. It makes this moment feel cosmic or weirdly aligned. It's always been my grandfather and my dad or my sisters and cousins, uncles, aunties, and friends around until now.

This will be a first for the both of us.

"Okay, I'll see you in a few days, granddaughter. Tell me when your travel is arranged."

Chapter 61

Dear Jeannine,

Remember that time your mother was living with you in Philly? You finally found a new place for y'all to stay near the bookshop. The next morning after you moved in, you ran to open the shop, when you got home that evening your mother was gone. You started freaking out because it was not like her to be out late at night, knowing she can't see. When she wasn't home by morning you was preparing to call the police when your younger sister, Number 3, called and said, guess who's back together? Who? Frick and Frack. A nickname for your two parents. Your dad, who was not even supposed to be driving, somehow got a car and drove all the way to Philadelphia to pick up your mother and then turned around and got back on the road and the two of them drove right back to his house. Neither ever said a thing to you about it. Of course and as per usual this didn't last and before the month was up they were back fighting or at least that's what you heard. While your mom was down in Virginia, somehow she had an emergency surgery, a retina transplant that restored her vision in one eye after twenty years. A miracle! She also divorced your dad, but they've been on again and off again forever. Wanna bet a divorce doesn't change that? Their love is blood-written, the type that stains the page, that hurts but never fades.

-j

Chapter 62

Lazarus calls me while I'm on the train to Virginia.

"Hey, Dad."

"So you're back in the game?"

"Yes, Dad."

I know that's his way of asking if I'm okay. "Aight, good." He's so Brooklyn. I wonder why he never asks me about what I'm writing. Or how Harvey is treating me. Or about feelings.

"You still trying to become mayor of Philadelphia?" he jokes.

"No, Dad, not trying to be the mayor of anything except myself." I've told him this many times.

"But you ain't never leaving Philly? Is you? Tell the truth. You ain't never leaving?"

"Dad, I am capable of leaving."

He cracks himself up. "No, you ain't. Remember you were interviewing the governor that one time. What's his name? Shapiro? Yeah. Josh Shapiro. How in the world, Jeannine, did you end up interviewing the damn governor of your state?"

"Well, we interviewed each other. His team asked me if we could interview each other on Instagram Live—the governor and me. At first I was gonna say no because politics. I'm allergic to it. But when I told them that they responded—'No, we really want you all to talk and connect so you can have an influence on the upcoming budget and adjoining small business policy.

We really think he needs to hear some of the things you have to say about books and small business and community. And we really want you to ask him questions, too. So, you both can grow.' Okay. I agreed."

"So, you just agreed?!" Lazarus is laughing and calling me funny even though I am not joking.

"Yeah, I agreed. The only stipulation was I was in Paris at my friend Marie's place—doing one of our writer's retreats—I was completing my book proposal. I told Shapiro's team if they didn't mind me interviewing him from Paris, then it would be okay. Marie would make the place beautiful with all of her flowers and colors and trinkets and things. And yeah, I had a live interview with Governor Shapiro about stories and letters and what the U.S. and Pennsylvania and Philadelphia could learn from Paris and France and Europe and vice versa. I called it the Jeannine and Josh Show in my head. I found an article about him starting a letter-writing campaign as a child to help another child when I was researching. We spoke about him being involved in the literary community. I bet writing has been passed down for generations in his family. I remind him of the power of words. I say, 'Josh, you're a word worker and I know that it doesn't go away.' I tell him he has a duty to protect and serve book people by any means. 'Ban the book bans,' I tell him. Designate bookshops as a part of cultural preservation and not just retail. Don't let big corporations swallow our industry. Reassess how we are taxed. Provide incentives for small businesses to collaborate and use shared resources. Watch out for book monopoly and censorship and illiteracy. Have more emergency funds for those small businesses getting started when you know most fail in the first five years. Give us each a business social worker. Allow us digital ways to track our tax dollars. Learn from the Fishtown BID, where I am on the board. Learn from Haddon Township Equity Initiative, where I am on the board. Come to Paris and see the way booksellers are protected and have their buildings passed down . . . booksellers need space!"

"There you go off on one of them tangents," my dad says.

"I know. . . ."

"But it's cool you met with him though. Spoke to him, let him have a piece of your mind. And all the way from Paris, 4,000 miles away, like you some fancy Baldwin type," he cracks himself up. "Well, I am glad you got your mojo back and your head is back on straight."

"How 'bout you? And Lester?" I ask.

"We're good, just here about to watch the Giants home game."

"Aight, Dad. See ya."

"Aight."

I get to Virginia and Nana has done just as I've asked. Lazarus doesn't suspect a thing (and neither does anyone else).

Chapter 63

What I love about Nana's house is that it never changes. The rack of different-colored teapots is still there next to the kitchen table, the glass curio with a gazillion glass trinkets inside is still there with everyone's photos from over the years still framed and over-packed, every face fighting for space in her display. My dad's army photo is still front and center. There's still a painting of my grandparents hanging on the wall, not drawn to proportion so their heads look a bit too small. It still smells like Nana's house—like everything is clean and coffee has been made and something just was baked. Everything is the same except for one thing.

Chapter 64

Dear Grandfather—

It's me Toni (aka Jeannine). I am in the back room of Nana's house writing the end of my book, but now I am taking a break. The mornings are too quiet without your singing and running to the bathroom while calling on your own name. "You can do it, Artie. You can make it." The evenings are too quiet without you yelling, "¡Ándale! ¡Ándale!" during Mets games. Nana is too quiet because she can't fuss with you like an Abbott and Costello routine. I hear you here, I see you here. But I miss you here. I never pictured a day without you here sitting in that chair next to Nana—your Choicy, your Pretty Girl, your Tubby Jack (Nana said don't ever let me hear you repeat that name—hehe!). I won't say it again. And because I never thought of losing our relationship, I took it for granted. Nana looks good though. Everything looks the same. I'm taking her to the doctor tomorrow and then over to the waterfront at Fort Monroe for ice cream to celebrate your anniversary. I know what everyone says, you're in a better place, but I can't imagine what place could be better than here with Nana's. Remember that time, I called myself not speaking to you all and you called me up and said, "Jeannine, never do that to me or my wife ever again"? I never did. Never will. I know what you're saying if you are reading this letter: Toni, finish your book. "¡Ándale! ¡Ándale!"

-jeannine

Chapter 65

Before I go to bed, Nana peeks into the back room. "Jeannine, I have something I have to say."

"Yes, Nana?"

I think she's coming here because I haven't showered in two days. I've been in the room not eating or sleeping and just writing—allowing myself to be out of this world. The back room is exactly what I need. Low light and stillness and endless tea. I feel safe in the back room. It's like my own cave.

She says, "Your Dad is really upset with me." And I can't tell if she's joking or if she's serious.

"Why?" I ask.

"Because he wants to know something that I can't tell him."

"What can't you tell him?"

"Who's taking me to the doctor tomorrow."

"Why . . . ?"

"Well usually your uncle takes me, right? So your dad asked me when your uncle would arrive and I said I wasn't able to answer that. But I also wasn't able to lie. So he sensed I was hiding something. But you asked me not to tell anyone you are in town. So he thinks I am keeping some big secret from him now."

"Nana, what kind of secret could you possibly be keeping from your grown son? Does he think you have a boyfriend or something?"

She laughs. "Jeannine, I am serious. He is saying some awful mess in these texts. He just doesn't like not knowing. He gets enraged. And . . ." she hesitates. "That's the thing, he asked me not to tell you some things as well. Which is making this even harder to explain."

"Nana. What?" Now I am upset, too.

"He asked me not to tell you that he's in the hospital."

"Why is Lazarus in the hospital this time?" I roll my eyes.

"Something went wrong with his surgery."

"Surgery?"

"Yeah. He asked me to keep that secret a few weeks ago, too."

"What?"

"Well, he had to get another amputation and he won't be able to use Lester. And I am only telling you this because now he is texting me some pretty awful mess. I'm not sure what to say. I will never show you these messages. But it's not something you should ever say to your mother."

I sit quietly. Close my computer. I can't tell if these two are pulling my leg or if they are both serious. They play too much.

"And what are you gonna do about it, Nana?"

"I'm gonna wish him a good night. Tell him I'll speak to him tomorrow."

I realize she's hurt. "I didn't mean to start stuff," I apologize. "I just . . . I'll surprise him at the hospital tomorrow after your doctor's appointment," I tell her. "It's all in the same complex, right?"

"Yeah, Sentura. But he doesn't like surprises."

I think he will laugh so hard at this one.

Nana thinks not.

The next morning, I continue writing while Nana is with her doctor. I practice making the grandmother in my novel the opposite of my nana in every way. My nana in real life would never curse or smoke weed. She's been an evangelist in the church since forever and a day (it's Southern slang, Harvey!).

Nana gets a perfect bill of health. She is doing everything right. Not taking any medicine. She eats well. And sleeps good. She's still walking, talking, and "in her right mind."

We leave her appointment and walk to the other wing of the hospital. I am winded. Nana is telling me I need to start taking vitamins.

I call my dad when we get to the hallway outside of his hospital room and he pretends everything is just fine. "Just getting ready to take my medicine," he says on the phone, not knowing me and Nana are standing outside of his room.

I knock.

He puts me on mute and yells, "Come in," thinking I'm a nurse or a doctor. "Come in," he yells again.

I push open the door slowly and when he sees me, a cat gets his tongue (Southern slang, Harvey!) and his mouth flies open. His face turns as white as a ghost. "Wha, wha, wha, what the hell, Jeannine?" he says. And Nana walks in behind me with her head hanging low. He gets tongue tied. I hang up my phone.

"Hey, Dad!" I say. He's thinner than the last time I saw him, but still looks good. His skin is taut and well moisturized. The last time I saw him it was me, him, and Number 3 hanging out at his house. They are each other's favorite. They love each other a lot. She rubs his legs and feet with moisturizer. It's beautiful and sacred and that's why they are each other's favorite, I think: they are completely vulnerable with each other in every way.

"You got me, you really got me," he laughs, bringing me back to reality. "For a second I thought you were a . . ."

"You looked like you saw something. It might have been your conscience, Dad."

"Oh, shut up," he laughs.

"You know you do have to apologize to Nana," I say.

He tries to change the subject to something that's wrong with his phone.

"Dad, it wasn't right what you said to her—what if it were the last thing you ever got to say?"

He mumbles, fumbles with his bedsheet and the remote control.

"Dad," I say a third time, "it was me who asked her to keep the secret."

"Yeah, but why would you not want me to know you was in town?"

"I just didn't want to be interrupted."

He smirks and jokes, "I shoulda known y'all was pulling my leg!"

We all laugh at his awfully timed dad joke. But it breaks the ice.

"But seriously though, Ma, I apologize," he finally says to my nana. "It won't happen again."

I think that apology was for more than a few texts. She accepts the apology and she apologizes, too. A lifetime of tension gets released in a few sentences.

"Look at her." He points at my grandmother. The picture of health. "Nobody here would believe that's my mother. I'm laid up here and she's over there."

We laugh throughout the afternoon, though he is also visibly in so much pain. He jokes about the hospital food, about losing his charger, about losing another part of his leg. He doesn't want any extra help. He's vulnerable, yet proud. He doesn't want me talking to the nurses. He doesn't want me changing his channel. He simply wants something for the pain. My nana prays over him, from the crown of his head to the sole of his foot. The nurses come and give him relief. They'll be discharging him home the next day. I promise I will get him home before I get on the road back to Philly for our next book event—Homegirls & Handgrenades.

"You think you so fancy with your champagne book events. Prob got y'all pinkies up while you chat." He tries to mock our hoity-toitiness but half the fingers on his hand are gone.

I tell them both that I can't stay out much longer. I am allergic to hospitals. It's easier to speak to him on the phone than to see him in person.

Before we leave, he asks me to tell the story of how I opened the bookshop again. I tell him I have another story about Number 1.

"Remember when Number 1 started walking around with one of Ma's large print leather bibles and a thick purple comforter? She listened to Prince and The New Power Generation's '7' on repeat. Sat in the dark in the hallway bathroom for hours by herself. She barely spoke. Before all of this, she used to be listening to alt that tapes on her pink stereo system. Creating her own mixtapes from hits on 103 Jamz. She used to decorate her room. Painted it blue herself. Stenciled her name in white letters onto the wall.

"But we weren't reading tall tales anymore. She was going somewhere new. She was sleeping in the hallway bathroom, and I was sleeping in the hallway outside of Ma's room.

"'Jeannine.' My older sister peeked with one eye from the dark bathroom.

"'Yes,' I responded through I-don't-want-to-sleep-alone tears.

"'Jeannine, I have to show you something. Something important,' she whispered through the black crack in the door.

"We are in this hot bathroom with the blanket over our heads sitting on the vent to fill her blanket with hot air like a balloon. My sister has Ma's emergency stash of tall candles lit around the bathroom and the bible open wide between her legs.

"'Blessed is he that readeth,' she began. She looked at me. Stopped. Waited as though she already knew what I didn't. Raised her eyebrows. Nodded as though she was shocked by what she'd found.

"'Okay, but we are girls.' I stuck my hands beneath my thighs on both sides.

"'That doesn't matter. Blessed is he that readeth revelations, Jeannine. There's mysteries in here, to be revealed.'

"'Oh, like "perhaps you can help solve these unsolved mysteries."' I pretended to understand.

"'And they that hear,' she whispered, pulling on my ear, 'the words of this prophecy keep those things which are written therein: for the time is at hand.'

"She slammed the book shut suddenly and we sat there by candlelight in silence. My sweaty palms sliding to find a place beneath my thighs. My heart backstroking through my stomach for no reason.

"'The time is at hand?' I got up, doe eyed and tipsy from the flickering lights. 'I don' get it.'

"She stood up, opened the door and pushed me out of the bathroom. 'The time is at hand, Jeannine,' she said, shutting the door in my face. My sister stayed in the bathroom reading by candlelight and I stayed awake lying on the carpet watching the lights dance beneath the door.

"'The time is at hand,' I heard a voice repeat in the back of my head. I covered it with both hands.

"These late-night rendezvous through Revelations would continue for a year. The voice continued way longer than that."

"Your sister had you reading Revelations as a little girl?" My dad laughs at my story. "Y'all were some strange kids. They been saying that since I was born. The time is always at hand," my dad laughs.

I go back home to the back room at Nana's house and write until I fall asleep at 42,703 words.

Chapter 66

The next day, I pick Lazarus up and drop him off at home from the hospital. We laugh because he says he can't wait to hang with his friends. I say I can't wait to hang with mine either.

I head back to Philly by train to host Alexis Pauline Gumbs's book event in my good sister-friend's backyard because there are way too many people registered to fit in the shop.

Alexis's work makes me ask myself: Do we choose ancestors, or do ancestors choose us?

I have seventy-five people who have registered for that I call Homegirls & Handgrenades in honor of Sonia Sanchez's ninetieth year. In my imagination it's a series that moves from home to home, celebrating Sanchez and her contemporaries through authors who write about them today, but I really need a producer for all the work that that will take. My sisters would be perfect partners but they've both grown up and I still want to play.

Today we are in a stone Victorian "mini-estate" in the Chestnut Hill section of Philadelphia. The menu includes champagne and gumbo as an ode to the literary Sisterhood formed by June Jordan and Alice Walker, which also included Margo Jefferson, Toni Morrison, Ntozake Shange, Philadelphia's own Vertamae Smart-Grosvenor, Audreen B. Ballard, and later Audre Lorde in the late seventies. They served this same dish fifty years ago to their sister-friends in a Manhattan apartment over literature, organizing, testimony, and conversation. According to literary historian Courtney Thorsson, members of the Sisterhood assert that it was not just writing or reading, but also having a strong literary community that contributed to their collective and individual success.

I've invited Alexis De Veaux to surprise interview Alexis Pauline Gumbs about her new book, a cosmo-biography called *Survival Is a Promise*. They both have written extensively about Lorde's work. Two decades ago, De Veaux was one of the first to write about Lorde through a humanizing biography called *Warrior Poet*.

De Veaux was a teacher, friend, and mentor of Gumbs—and now both are literary titans in their own right sitting in my good sister-friend's backyard.

One Alexis's work is an extension of the other Alexis who came before her—while both are an extension of the good Lorde, like a spectrum reflecting each other's light, we bounce off one another.

The conversation hops around a lot, but it keeps coming back to veneration. How do our ancestors wish to be honored and remembered? But also, how do we want to be honored and remembered when we become ancestors?

It's a magical fall evening with a full moon and a soft breeze that we call Audre when it blows against the wind chimes.

I wish I could make this an ongoing series, my entrepreneur self says.

Run by who? my writer self asks with a side-eye. *You don't need to do another thing*, my writer self continues, knowing that to host this one event my entrepreneur self had to design the graphics, build the ticketing system, and promote, promote, promote. Have multiple meetings with both Alexises and their teams, and meetings with my sister-friend whose house this is, and arrange travel, and handle customer service, and hire a chef, and design the menu, and bring all of the glassware (because she can't serve people off of plastic), and order the books, and order the chairs, and arrange the flowers, and set up the house, and . . .

Yet my entrepreneur self continues, saying she would just love it if folks let us take over their homes and we invite their favorite author to the house and then their favorite author's friends. Then we get to surprise the author with a conversation partner. We get to hire a chef and curate a coordinating menu and an amazing cleaning staff to swoop in. And in exchange for hosting my homegirls, the homegirl whose house it is gets leftovers, signed books, and a clean home. We make just enough to do it all again.

My writer self sighs. My entrepreneur self sighs too.

My phone rings but I do not pick up. It's a whirlwind of an evening with yellow roses and candles placed everywhere throughout my friend's home and yard—*you can create a bookshop anywhere*, I remind myself. Gumbs (and the entire audience) nearly jump out of their seats when I announce that someone is coming from around the corner as our surprise guest interviewer. I've been hiding DeVeaux in a back room while folks eat, mix, and mingle. When DeVeaux walks out the two make a full embrace. We are watching history get made.

The two Alexises and all who attend are blown away by the night and the perfect fall weather, the gumbo, the mugs, the tote bags, and the love among sister-friends that is different than any other kind of love.

I orchestrate for several poets to pop up randomly throughout the evening and break into unexpected warrior poems. At intervals throughout the talk, I have an a capella group stand to lead us in soulful songs. Toward the end we all sing Sweet Honey in the Rock's "Ella's Song" together with the Audre Lorde wind chimes singing along. My phone rings. I do not pick up. Just as we finish for the night, it begins to drizzle and everyone starts racing around to help clean up.

I'm putting up the last chairs when I get a message: "Your dad lost consciousness." My phone rings. I do not pick up.

"What in the fuck?" I say out loud and take a seat.

I curse so loud, I interrupt a group of sister-friends chatting in front of me. One of them turns around and asks me what's wrong. I show her the text message to make sure I'm reading it right. She reads it out loud. She makes me stand up and follow her into the kitchen. She makes me drink water out of my mug. I must look dazed or confused because several other sister-friends form a line in the kitchen and wrap their arms around me, one by one.

It's beautiful and sacred, but I don't understand why they are doing it. I am numb. I don't need hugs, I need to finish cleaning up.

My sister-friends don't know my dad is Lazarus. They don't know he can walk on water. He always comes back. He always gets up. This is not a time for mourning, it's the time for miracles.

I finish hosting like nothing is going on. I stay until everyone has left with their signed books and their mugs that say Homegirls & Handgrenades. I stay until I clean up all the chairs and dishes and food and flowers. I stay until I can't stay any longer. My sister-friend's children have school in the morning.

In my car, I call my dad's phone thinking he's probably popped up already, but no answer. He must have lost his charger (again!).

Chapter 67

I get a call the next day from the nurse at Sentara Hospital. "Your dad's awake," she says.

"See, I told you he always gets back up," I tell my older cousin Jalla who is visiting me for the week. She's here to ladysit me so I can finish this last chapter of my book and to teach me how to run a café.

"But he had some issues answering questions like his name and where he was," the nurse continues.

"Yeah, he gets like that sometimes," I say. It was probably from the medicine. "He'll be fine."

"Well..."

"Well, tell him to call me when he gets up."

I beg my cousin to make me a Trini-style fry bake. It's a dough that gets tossed around and manhandled and then left out to rise. It rises even more when it hits the hot oil.

"Miracles, I say. I see them all of the time. That should be the end of the book," I laugh. "But what does that even mean?"

I complain to Jalla that I don't know how to end my novel and I wish I could just wrap it all in one sentence. I don't see an ending in sight. I know the end of the story, but I don't know how to get there.

Jalla says pleasant things that people always say, like *it'll come to you. Listen to your intuition. All will be well. Everything is unfold-*

ing in perfect order. But day after day I hover at 47,892 words, not sure how to find the resolution to a story that I love so much that I don't want to see it come to an end.

Lazarus calls.

"Hey, Dad."

"Hey . . ." He starts laughing uncontrollably like he's sipping helium. So much so that I start laughing uncontrollably, too.

"Dad? Hey!"

But now he cannot stop laughing, so Jalla is laughing and I'm laughing. We are all laughing.

"Dad? Why are we laughing?" I ask him, still laughing.

"Because I can't feel anything!" He's cracking up so much, heehees and hahas and hollers through his teeth. You know, the kind of laugh where tears come down and your right side hurts. I'm laughing like that too. Doubled over belly-busting laughter at nothing.

"Well, that's good." I finally catch my breath and wipe my laughter tears.

"You see, me and you," he laughs, "we are funny," he tells me, catching his breath. "Keep making people laugh, Jeannine."

"Yeah, Dad. Okay!" I try not to start laughing again.

His nurse comes in and he has to do whatever things the nurses always make him do. Scrub. Rinse. Steam. Repeat.

"I'll call you in the morning, Dad."

"Okay," he says, still cracking up. "But please tell your mom to call me ASAP. I know you don't like being in the middle, but I need you to do this for me."

"Okay, Dad," I hesitate.

I hang up laughing like, *damn he must be high as hell.* I eat Jalla's fried bakes and drink tea and laugh about cousin things.

Chapter 68

NOTE TO SELF:

Dear Jeannine,

Remember the time you called your mom and asked her to call your dad. Then y'all hung up. You wanted to cry but you laughed from your funny bone. This is your reminder to release it.

    You will forever wonder if she called him. But deep down you know she did. You're so caught up in their love story. You always have been.

Signed,
Number 2

SECTION IV:
OCTOBER 2024

Jeannine A. Cook interviews Marie Brown

JEANNINE A. COOK: I am scared and don't know what to do.

MARIE BROWN: It's all going to be amazing.

Chapter 69

A woman calls me the next day and says she thinks it's time for me to come to the hospital to pay my last respects, but they don't know my dad is Lazarus. I've said goodbye many times. I just play along. I fly to Virginia. All I have is my purse and my notebook. I land and head straight to the hospital.

I take feverish notes as I sit next to my father's hospital bed listening to him snore. I believe there's still a chance I can make it to the book festival the next day to interview Lorene Cary, since he'll wake up any minute. I know him.

I let the audiobook of Lorene Cary reading *Ladysitting* play loud in the hospital room as I read along. Her voice is on in the background for hours. She makes my dad's unbearable snoring more bearable.

After several hours of him just snoring, he snaps out of his deep sleep and jumps up out of nowhere.

I stop writing.

Lazarus is back.

I knew it.

My dad sits up and yells, "WOW!" at the top of his falsetto lungs.

"Wow what, Dad?!" I laugh. "It's Lorene, right?" I ask. "It's a really good book."

Then he lies back down and goes back to snoring. I go back to my notebook.

Chapter 70

NOTE TO SELF:

One day you're gonna want to remember this, it smells sterile in here, too, like hospital sheets, you're going to want to write this out of yourself, it'll make a great story about how your dad would die and come back to life—candles, priests, last rites and all, and you can tell your children's children's children's children so they know about miracles and their own family lore. You jot down everything you see and hear and voices that aren't there and thoughts and prayers and ideas and poems. You just keep writing. Keep writing because one day you're gonna want to read these notes.

Chapter 71

A few hours later the audiobook of *Ladysitting* that we are listening to ends with Lorene after her nana's funeral and I have to run to the bathroom to breathe. I feel funny like I am being washed down the drain. I weep for Nana Jackson, though she's lived past a hundred in the book. She's lived a full life that was very long. And I have read this story many times before. I know how it ends. I cry hard for her even though I know she's dying from the very beginning. For two whole minutes I let it all out, snot and moans and aches, and then splash water on my face. "Keep your head in the game," I say out loud. And think I've pulled myself together. But I can't. And I let loose again.

"Why is no one here with me?!" I ask myself in the mirror.

No response.

When I run back into the hospital room from the bathroom, someone is there with me. It is my older cousin Tresserlyn. She is in a chair sitting across from my dad. She's appeared out of nowhere like an aberration. She says "something" told her to stop by. She was supposed to be headed out of town and doubled back.

She asks me how the bookshops are doing, and I just laugh.

She is speaking loudly and wants to sing to my dad. He and I want to listen to my audiobook (again!). I don't want to listen to her. I restart the book from the beginning.

A beautiful big bootie nurse comes in and rubs his head and kisses his hand. She tells me she's Nurse Erika, that she is not his nurse tonight, but they've been close for many years. I read between the lines as she rubs his arm and hugs on him. I want to hug her like she's my mother, but she is not, so I nod my head and stare.

You still got it, Dad. You've made your point. You can get the ladies no matter what.

Just get up now so we can go home.

My cousin Tresserlyn starts singing off key to my dad as his nurse girlfriend leaves. I don't love her singing, but she proceeds:

Wade in the water, wade in the water children, wade in the water, God's gonna trouble the water.

Then she wants to tell me about our family tree, as she sings. I am preoccupied. She says this is a tradition that's being passed down to me and I need to listen:

Wade in the water, wade in the water children, wade in the water, God's gonna trouble the water.

I want to write and doodle and scratch in my notebook and listen to Lorene. I want to crawl in a ball under the bed. Ms. Harriett where are you? Ms. Ida? Ms. Josephine? I want to eat ice cream. Teach a class. Ride a horse. Anything.

Tresserlyn cuts her eyes and tells me it's important that I listen, so I turn off the audiobook and she begins.

God's gonna trouble the water.

"This is a story that begins with our great-grandparents, Henry Reese and Thomasina Commander," she tells me. She's so loud I can't understand why she's yelling. *Brooklyn people are so loud*, I think. My dad is gonna love that joke when he wakes up. "Henry Reese lived to be ninety-six years old and passed on July 17, 2012."

God's gonna trouble the water.

"Thomasina Commander-Reese lived a long life and passed in March of '86. Jeannine, it was Thomasina who told us when you were born you had a gift even though she was going blind."

God's gonna trouble the water.

"Thomasina and Henry begot your grandmother, Nancy May Reese."

God's gonna trouble the water.

"And her sister, my mother, your great-aunt, Dorothy Reese, who passed away on January 25, 2021." Saying this makes Tresserlyn's voice crack.

God's gonna trouble the water.

"And our uncle Robert Lee, who passed on June 1, 2024."

"Nancy met James Cook and they begot your father, James Anthony Cook, who we called Anthony. Your father's father passed away in 1959. Nancy remarried Arthur Dunbar and together they raised Anthony until Arthur passed away on December 23, 2023."

I don't understand why she wants to tell me information that I already know.

God's gonna trouble the water.

"And today is October 2, 2024."

God's gonna trouble the water.

"Today is your father's day."

God's gonna trouble the water.

I realize his snoring has stopped as my dad's phone rings.

All my bones are funny bones.

I wish my dad would answer his damn phone.

Chapter 72

NOTE TO SELF:

Remember that time you had to take Lester to Nana's house and tell her that her firstborn son was gone? You handed her his prosthetic leg, and said, "Nana, that's all."

You couldn't bring yourself to call your mom or your sisters or your cousins or friends. So, Nana must have made the calls. You still can't remember.

That night your voice went ghost. You had nothing nice to say so you said nothing at all.

Chapter 73

The next morning my entrepreneur self is ambivalent and still going strong. She is able to write a business letter, not to Ms. Harriett or Ms. Josephine or herself, but to Lorene:

```
Dear Dr. Lorene Cary & Book Festival Committee—

I regret to inform you that I cannot make it to
today's book festival for my interview with Dr.
Cary because last night my father passed away.
   Thank you in advance for understanding that I
am in so much pain that I can't breathe.

                        Yours in community,
                        Jeannine A. Cook
```

Chapter 74

My writer self is strong in a different way; she writes to my editor and my agent:

Dear Abby & Marie,

My deepest apologies, as you know, life (and death) came at me like a high-speed train these last few weeks and I'm so thankful to be surrounded by folks like you all as these changes continue to unfold. I appreciate the love and see its power in a renewed light.

I also know it's important to stay grounded and present to move the book projects forward on time. I'm honestly eager for the distraction (and hopeful healing) of the writing process.

I've been reading the foreword to Toni Morrison's *Song of Solomon* on repeat as she discusses the ways that losing her father shifted her and her writing and then helped to craft her book. I'm praying for a similar transformation. Though at some moments that hope seems silly.

That said, it is my strong desire that we can reschedule our meeting to discuss the current book project and keep the project on track for its November deadline.

   I appreciate you both for taking the time with and for me. And like my nana always says, "I believe I'll run on and see what the end's gonna be."

                                Much love.
                                Jeannine
Everything is unfolding in perfect order

Chapter 75

Harvey comes knocking again and again for weeks, and then one day I finally open the bookshop door. I have successfully been hiding and sleeping behind the bar.

"You should stay active," he says, opening the windows. "At least get some air."

"No, YOU should stay active," I mumble.

I ignore him and walk back behind the bright blue bar, where I have a little place to sleep on the floor. Air won't stop me from suffocating. I don't want to hear anyone's voice or for anyone to have to smell my breath. I can't recall the last time I brushed my teeth or washed myself. I would rather feel nothing, which is working because I haven't felt anything in days.

Harvey puts a blanket on me as I lie back down on the bookshop floor. "No, thank you," I say, pushing it away.

"Hold it," he says. "Before you drop it."

"Hold what?" I'm tired and I just want to sleep. I'm dozing off when out of the blanket crawls a shivering black-and-white puppy. He tiptoes up my chest to my chin and tries to lick my face.

"Harvey, what is this?" I say, trying to hand him the tiny dog.

"A life."

"He looks like a mouse." This puppy is obviously too small to be away from his mother. "Or a premature rat." His eyes are barely open, he has no teeth, and he cannot really walk. "Was he born yesterday?" I say, holding his wrinkled body in the palm of my hand.

"I think he's two weeks old. I was at the grocery store this morning and a woman was standing outside begging, crying that she needed medicine for her baby. She held out her cup but instead of asking for money she was showing me a tiny baby puppy. She said she could not afford to raise this little guy, so I gave her the money for the medicine and took the dog. But something tells me he's yours."

"He's not . . ." I start to say, then soften. For a few seconds I feel anger, which is better than the ache. "What's his name?" I say, trying to tuck the small animal beneath my shirt so he stops shivering.

Harvey says, "His name is Jac. J-A-C—no K. Isn't that how they spell it in Paris?"

"Harvey, that's my dad's name. And no, that's not how they spell Jack in French."

"I thought you said your dad's name was Lazarus."

"His initials—James Anthony Cook. J-A-C. Jac."

"Exactly," Harvey says, like he's known that all along.

I give him a side-eye, not sure whether he's pulling my leg. "And what if Jac Jac dies on me? Did you think what that might do to me?" I say looking at the underdeveloped dog.

"What if he lives? Did you think what that might do to you?"

"You're not listening to me."

"Just get up and take care of lil' Jac Jac." Harvey winks. "He needs you. And you need him."

Harvey hands me a teeny baby bottle, a tin of powdered milk, and a vial of honey. "If his sugar drops just rub a bit of honey on his gums and he'll be okay." I place a bit of honey on my own gums, trying to remember what sweetness tastes like. Jac Jac lies still beneath my shirt, and I think the worst. He's dead already. "How am I supposed to know if his sugar drops?"

"Use your instincts."

When Harvey leaves, I lie still trying to feel Jac Jac's faint heartbeat against my own. He and I feel just the same—like we're barely holding on.

Chapter 76

One month later, Jac Jac and I are sitting in Harriett's, except now I've bathed and doused us both with a bit of holy water. The walls are complete, paint is finished, the shelves are hung. Jac Jac has grown some, but he's still small enough to fit in the front pocket of my denim overalls.

I have my laptop open in front of me as I reread my manuscript for the millionth time.

Jac Jac is a tiny ball of energy. He jumps out of my pocket and down onto my computer. He wants to play . . . or go to the bathroom. He climbs up and sits on my keyboard. And makes the cutest little face. "You better not pee . . ." I tell him, laughing at my own joke. I put him down on the floor just in case.

I sip a cup of mint tea and finally press send on the first draft of my first novel, *It's Me They Follow*, at 50,345 words.

I close the laptop, and my eyes feel like they are glued shut as I take in the silence of being done.

"You finally got that story up out you, huh?!" Lazarus jokes from the other side, and I hear a whole host of voices laugh with him.

The End.

Postscript

Dear Tainty Lorene,

I need a quiet place to write my next book. It's a memoir. It's overdue and I am late again.

                        - jeannine

Shugs,

Want to use my office?

                        -Tainty

Dear Tainty Lorene,

Yes. Yes. That's exactly what I need. A room of my own.

                        -jeannine

Post Postscript

Hello, Dr. Hahn.

Yes, Jeannine.

I think I am ready for my next chapter.

///

Acknowledgments

To my Nana, Nancy May, thank you for being our matriarch.

To my mother, Heather, may you continue to see through the darkness and walk into the marvelous light. I will write a story all about the miracle that is you someday just as I have promised.

To my children, Messiah, Jenesis, and Anais for sharing me with the world and sacrificing so much. I do it for you and my great-great-grandchildren, a lineage that will come through you, though we may never meet. And to my bonus children—Brianna, Brayiona, Faith, Seraiah, Aunye, and the youth conductors, remember you already have the greatest love of all.

To my aunties, Phillis, Janice, Ann Marie, Jeannine, Dorrques, Karen, Freda, Lucille, and Neicy for being the best role models. And to my cousins, especially Jalla, Petrina, Kymone, Kuan, Tresserlyn, Darlene, Inesha, Dashawn, Keverette, and Shaniece, who have shown up for me majorly in this season.

To my sisters, Jazzy and Jenielle, thank you for letting me squeeze between you two once upon a time.

ACKNOWLEDGMENTS

Thank you to my literary family, Marie Brown my agent extraordinaire, Abby West my visionary editor, Makayla, Tara, Ashley, Alyssa, Judith, Stephen, Sekou, and the entire Amistad/HarperCollins family for helping me to birth a book (or two).

To my guides Sannii, Ms. Donna, Mr. Stephen, Nomi, Lorene, Marie, Tayyib, Sara, Dyana, Claire, Sekayi, Dr. Mo, Cin, David, Jack, Unc, and Camille, thank you for never giving up, even though guiding me must be quite the task.

To my Dadas Maria, Lucy, Lolo, Sophie, Jibek, and Nadya you make love real.

To my friends Vashti, Misty, Charlotte, Starfire, Elizabeth, Andrea, Blew, Pheralyn, Karen, Isis, Becky, Carrie, Pip, Brendan, Bryan, Manny, Tameika, Tifah, Tonia, Tammy, Sharon, Adachi, Bill, Jean Jacque, Cymande, Thalia, and Tracy for helping me to breathe and laugh and breathe again.

To my habibi, Harvey, and the entire Schmidt family, thank you all for pouring into me in the many ways that you do.

To my fellow Shopkeepers, I know it is not easy, but may you do it with ease.

To the community always. You know how much you mean to me.

To my many literary godmothers, especially Sonia Sanchez, Alice Walker, and Nikki Giovanni, for being in conversation with me.

And to my ancestors, may my good deeds add onto yours.